D0874437

MAY 1968
RECEIVED
OCEAN COUNTY
COLLEGE LIBRARY
TOMS RIVER, N. J.

THE UNIVERSITY OF MISSOURI

STUDIES

VOLUME XXIX

Swan, Cygnets, and Owl

AN ANTHOLOGY OF MODERNIST POETRY IN SPANISH AMERICA

Translations by

MILDRED E. JOHNSON

With an Introductory Essay by

J. S. BRUSHWOOD

1956

The University of Missouri Studies

Columbia, Missouri

Library of Congress Catalog Card No. 56-12576

Address Communications to

EDITOR, UNIVERSITY OF MISSOURI STUDIES
UNIVERSITY OF MISSOURI
COLUMBIA, MISSOURI

Price $4.00

PRINTED IN THE UNITED STATES OF AMERICA

To the Memory

of

JACOB WARSHAW

PREFACE

Since this work treats of Spanish-American poetry from about 1885 to 1936, it has been impossible to include poems by all poets of merit. It has been necessary to choose rather arbitrarily at times, especially in the contemporary period, but an attempt has been made to include representative works of each period as far as possible. I was unable to get in touch with some of the contemporary poets, and one major poet, Gabriela Mistral, refused to authorize the use of her poems.

In my translations I have attempted to reproduce the ideas and imagery expressed in the original without omitting any or adding any of my own. A freer translation would probably be more artistic but would lack fidelity. I have also attempted to employ the same verse form with the fewest possible modifications. For instance, I have frequently replaced Spanish feminine lines with the more common English masculine lines; otherwise, I have usually employed the same number of syllables in each verse as in the Spanish. I have reproduced the Spanish rhyme scheme in many poems, but in others I have replaced assonance with consonantal rhyme or blank verse, or have rhymed only the even lines, preferring not to sacrifice the sense of the poem to the exigencies of rhyme. In short, I have attempted to make my translations as faithful to the original Spanish poems as is linguistically possible.

The chronological limits of this anthology extend beyond the dates usually assigned to the end of Modernism proper. It is hoped that the more recent poetry will demonstrate the effect of Modernism on subsequent poetic expression.

Grateful acknowledgment is made of the courtesy of poets and of the heirs of deceased poets who have granted permission to translate and publish poems used in this anthology, and who have expressed their interest in the work.

M. E. J.

Contents

An Introductory Essay on Modernism

An Introductory Essay on Modernism

The poetry of a particular place, or of a particular time may possess certain distinguishing characteristics which afford it the dignity of a name all its own. These characteristics, if each one be considered separately, may not be confined to the particular time nor to the particular place, but may be identified with that time and place because of the peculiar perspective in which they are seen. The perspective may be the result of the common physical or spiritual needs of the artists, or of an inclination to conform to some arbitrary standard of what is proper, or of an attempt to discover successful expression by imitation of successful expression, or even by a rather haphazard use of techniques and materials found in other places in the search for a road.

The basis of Spanish-American poetic expression is well within the Hispanic tradition and that tradition is in turn within the European tradition. It is important, and sometimes surprising to those who are unacquainted with Spanish-American literature, to recognize that the same general cultural movements occur in Spanish America as occur in the rest of the western world. That is to say that allowing for differences of a few years one way or the other, Spanish-American literary expression has been Neo-classic when European expression was Neo-classic, romantic when European expression was romantic, and so on. Progressing from this large generalization to a more specific one, it should be recognized that Spanish-American literature has differed generally in much the same way that Spanish expression has differed. Some of these Hispanic peculiarities are: a fundamentally realistic view of life which tempered the extremes of the Romantic Movement and gave a special meaning to Realism; the consideration of Neo-classicism as a necessary burden required by good taste; a particular religious faith so integral a part of the culture that Naturalism was never fully accepted; and a set of social and economic circumstances which are the source of questions not only of social justice but of social welfare, which in turn are the cause of artistic preoccupation with social problems. Spanish-American expression has in its turn deviated in certain respects from the Hispanic tradition in spite of the fact that its roots are well within it. The most noticeable deviation from the Hispanic came with the political independence of Spanish America, when the American writers reached toward influences other than the Spanish in an attempt to find their own expression.

Political independence came to Spanish America as a part of the general liberal movement which brought independence to the United States, and which was the motivation of the French revolution. The independence movement in Spanish America was a movement sponsored by intellectuals, not by the lower classes. The general ideology of these leaders was developed under the influence of French thought, especially that of Jean Jacques Rousseau. At first this revolutionary ideology was something of an intellectual toy and it might be said with some justification that the leaders were shocked by the fact of the French revolution. When, however, Napoleon's imperial designs left the Americas without a Spanish king, they found that they could hardly maintain a status quo which did not exist. Ideology was translated into action and the independence movement lasted from 1810 to 1824. This same period marks a period of transition from Neo-classicism, such as it had been in Spanish America, to Romanticism. As soon as it became apparent that new nations were in the making, political thinkers began searching for appropriate forms of government and writers started on the long road toward the discovery of new national expression. Neither political thought nor literary production was able for many years to achieve the independence that each sought, largely because neither the one nor the other could fully understand the problems and necessities of the Spanish-American nations. While there was creative thought, there was incomplete vision, and a large part of the nineteenth century is a history of imitations, often unsuccessful, which were the result of trying to adapt certain foreign materials or forms or ideas to the American situation. It is quite natural that, since the intellectual activity of the time was already inspired by and oriented toward French culture, the Spanish Americans should be inclined to accept France as a cultural mother, replacing Spain. It would be hard indeed to place too much emphasis on the fact that this acceptance of France as a source of cultural inspiration does not mean a denial of the Hispanic tradition. Quite to the contrary, the foundations of the Hispanic-American literary expression remain within the Hispanic tradition and evidence of this fact persisted throughout all the years of even the greatest French influence. Nor should it be understood that the only foreign influence was France. Influences coming from England and Germany can be found also. Spanish-American intellectuals, however, could more often read French than they could read German or English, and therefore the very practical necessity of a skill enhanced a natural tendency toward another Latin country. It must be remembered that they were attempting to find in all these cultural sources a means of expressing something which was typically American.

The "something" which the Americans were trying to express is not easily defined. Some of them unquestionably sensed their new nationality and wished to verbalize the feeling. Others posed behind a trenchant political nationalism which was more a matter of assumed pride than deep feeling. Spanish-American poetry during the early years of the Romantic Period was usually either historical or a treatment of nature which in some way identified natural phenomena with the course of human life or the gamut of human emotions. The "Americanism" contained in this poetry was historical event or description of natural scenery which certainly provided identity with America, but which had little to do with the deeper feelings which might be said to have comprised the American feeling. There are elements which by strength of fact are associated with the New World, but during the Romantic Period these elements are rarely more than suggestions of fuller development which came later: the Indian and his bravery and nobility, the mestizo as a social problem, the vastness of the Argentine pampa, and the isolation of certain sections of America. These elements were treated in a fashion which might just as well have been French as American. There was in general no genuine identification of the American author with American themes. The best poetry of the Romantic Period was the gaucho poetry of Argentina, which did manage to capture the spirit of a section and of a kind of people which belonged only to America. The success of gaucho poetry is the result of its close relationship with the basic Hispanic reality which was able to see men in the smallness of their daily existence, in spite of Romantic overstatement. Poetry in general during the Romantic Period changed gradually from historical poetry and poetry of nature to a display of maudlin sentimentality either amatory or domestic.

It has been said that the Spanish-American way of thinking is particularly congenial to Romantic exaggeration. To a certain extent this is true, because Spanish-American expression tends toward the dramatic and often toward the noise and violence that are frequently associated with Romanticism. Emotional expression is more general in Spanish America than it is in the United States. Poetry and sentimentality are considered by many to constitute almost a phase in an individual's development. Poetry, therefore, continues to be identified usually with the expression of emotional pain or joy, usually amatory. The best Spanish-American poetry, of course, rises above this level either by giving sentiment depth or by broadening the poetic vision. There is no doubt, however, that the characteristics which immediately attract the attention of the reader are its emotional overstatement and its endless repetition of the same idea.

One way of stating the difference between Spanish-American Romantic poetry and the following Modernist poetry is to say that it is the difference between imitation of a model and the regeneration of a model's influence through a creative act. Some critics have said that the Spanish-American Modernist poets studied and accepted the techniques and ideas of certain French poets and made these techniques and ideas a part of their own expression. Certainly this view is accurate, but it is limited. It does not state the tremendous importance of the Hispanic tradition in Modernist poetry, nor does it indicate the nationalistic tendencies that are evident in the works of the Modernists. As a matter of fact, it is much more difficult to state a series of characteristics common to Spanish-American Modernist poets than it is to do so for French Symbolism or for French Parnassianism or for the English pre-Raphaelites. Rather than regard the Modernists as a school, it is better to regard them as poets motivated to seek a new way of expression by the same progress toward intellectual independence. Modernism really means leaving off imitation of models and understanding the creative act. The special and sometimes individual characteristics of this process are secondary to the primary fact, although they may be more readily evident. Such an understanding of Modernism will explain its relationship to Romanticism, to the Hispanic tradition, to the various French schools, and will make clear the continuity of the poetic tradition into what has been foolishly called post-Modernism. Post-Modernism differs from Modernism as a result of changed secondary characteristics, rather than of changed primary characteristics. It will perhaps be clearer to most readers to explain Modernist poetry by a statement of three effects that it has exercised in Spanish-American literary development, rather than by talking about a long list of specific and variable characteristics. These three generalized statements as to what Modernist poetry has been are: 1. A refinement of Romantic expression. 2. A reaction against Realism. 3. A coming of age in Spanish-American poetry.

1. A Refinement of Romantic Expression

There is, of course, no real point of beginning for Modernist poetry. One wanders from the overly neat classification of precursors of Modernism, Modernists and post-Modernists to an overly generalized acceptance of all Modernism as a continuation of Romanticism. The difference between the so-called precursors of Moderism (Martí, Gutiérrez Nájera, Silva, Casal, and sometimes González Prada) and those usually considered real Modernists is largely a matter of degree. That is to say, all of these precursors show in their works at least one of the characteristics generally associated with Modernism, but may not and usually do not show as many of the characteristics as those who are called Modernists proper. In the case of Martí, for example, the only real departure from typical Romantic poetry is his simplicity. Martí's exaggeration, his subjectivity, his direct and obvious statement, are all Romantic in nature; but his verses are short, complete ideas which are quite different from the wandering repetition of the Romantic Period. This tendency to simplify might be called one of the characteristics of Modernism. It is certainly one of the reliefs from Romanticism. Simplicity and brevity in the poems of Martí, and in some of the poems of González Prada, are perhaps the result of the particular attitudes of these men toward the writing of poetry. Neither Martí nor González Prada would have considered himself primarily a poet. Though they were men much concerned with the social and political problems of their countries, their poetry is really the expression of their most basic feelings, of the very human and very natural emotions that belong to them as ordinary men rather than as public figures. Poetry is, therefore, their particular way of clinging to the reality of their existence as men. Simplicity as a characteristic of Modernism certainly does not exist for a similar reason in the works of all the Modernist poets. Rather it is a result of reaction against a literary style which had become tired.

During the Modernist period in Spanish America, the poets looked mainly to France for inspiration, just as they had done in the preceding period, and it was this source of inspiration which was translated into their own terms through their own creative act. Other influences such as the pre-Raphaelite influence from England came for the most part through France. The French poetry which was influential among the Modernists was of two kinds, Parnassian and Symbolist. These two schools of poetry are not entirely congenial with each other, and it would be difficult to see how both of them could be characteristic of a school of poetry. It is only by assuming that Modernism is not a school of poetry, but an attitude toward writing poetry that the coexistence of Parnassianism and Symbolism makes sense.

As absurd as it may seem superficially, it is necessary to speak of a certain classic tendency within the limits of a period which we shall contend is basically Romantic. This classic tendency resides in the Parnassian preoccupation with form. To say that the Parnassians preferred the sonnet to other forms of poetry will give the reader some indication of their interest. Their preoccupation with form had as a corollary a perfectionist drive which was inclined to make their poetry coldly beautiful. It was, as matter of fact, a rather objective poetry. The idea was not as important as the carved result. Parnassianism as the Spanish Americans understood it reinforced their adherence to a cult of beauty and enabled them to seek refuge in beauty for its own sake. Perhaps the best example of Parnassian influence in the present volume is Darío's "The Swan," which is interesting not only because of its perfection of form, but also because it is in the nature of a poetic manifesto. The author's declaration is not a complete expression of the principles of Modernism, but "The Swan" serves very well as an indication of how Parnassianism joined with Symbolism in influencing the Modernist movement.

Symbolism is more comprehensive than Parnassianism in that it is the result of the play of a larger portion of the artist's creative self. While Parnassianism concerned itself mainly with the satisfaction of creating a chiseled perfection, Symbolism is an attempt to communicate a feeling which is the result of an infinite variety of emotional and sensory responses. The object of Symbolist poetry is, therefore, not concentrated toward one purpose like perfection of form, but is the expression of any or many of an endless variety of feelings. While Parnassianism tends toward the objective, Symbolism is completely subjective, and the two are in this sense opposed to each other. It would be wrong to give the impression that the Symbolist was in no way concerned with form. True enough, form is not of primary importance and, in the work of some poets, is of next to no importance. But in the work of a number of writers, form as a complement to the audio-suggestion of Symbolism has a special meaning. A case in point is Silva's "Nocturne." Although the poem follows no classic form and achieves no classic beauty of form, there is no doubt that the author was keenly conscious of the form of his work and of its significance in the communication of his feeling. The sobbing short lines, the sudden rush of ideas and associations in the long lines, the futile expectancy of the indented, slanted lines and repetition, all contribute to the total feeling of the poem. Such freedom in the use of form was common enough among the Modernists, though hardly more common than the stricter interpretation of form in the Parnassian sense. The other characteristics of Symbolism combined both with the understanding of form as in the case of Silva, and with the understanding of form in the Parnassian sense.

The particular things that the Symbolists did in their poems may be understood more easily if their motivation be stated first. The Symbolist wished to communicate a feeling which he could not verbalize within the limits of ordinary poetic language. The Romantics and the Parnassians spoke of things and circumstances as they were, and as they could be described for reception by the reader. Although the reader might be puzzled as to the whole implication of the poem, or as to certain possible interpretations, he always knew what, basically, the poet was talking about; that is to say, the reader, although he might not understand the work of the Romantic or the Parnassian fully, would be able to describe the work by saying that the poet is writing about such and such thing. Such a situation is not always true of the Symbolists. Since they were trying to communicate a response that could not be verbalized easily, often even their general intent is obscure; and in order to enjoy the poetry of the Symbolists, the reader must be willing to allow his imagination complete freedom and not limit his potential emotional response. It should be made quite clear that the response needed for reception of the Symbolist communication is an emotional one, not an intellectual one. Such confusion has frequently associated Symbolist poetry with some contemporary poetry which demands a similar though even more intense participation on the part of the reader in order that the creative communication may be completed. The latter kind of expression is a much more profound revelation of the truth of one's self than is the communication of impressions by the Symbolists. It is, indeed, a spontaneous expression which has passed through intellectualization and has become a more fundamental part of the artist then the relatively immediate response of the Symbolist. This poetic motivation will be seen in a few of the most recent works in this anthology and will demand some additional comment later on.

Turning to the Symbolist's problem of communicating his impression, let us re-state the problem and discover what particular techniques the poet uses in order to achieve the communication. The poet observes something which impresses him one way or another. We as readers are not yet concerned about how it impresses him, but we must understand that the answer to the question "how" will embody an expression of his emotions and physical feelings at the time he received the impression. The problem, then, is to find a means of communicating these responses or of creating these responses in his reader. Now it is true that the poet can never be entirely sure that he will have created precisely the same set of responses in his reader that have been created in him, but then neither can any writer be entirely sure that his words will be interpreted by any reader in precisely the same way that they are understood by him.

The Symbolist's problem differs from the problem of other writers mainly as to degree, and he has had to seek special techniques in order to accomplish his purpose. His technique has identified his kind of poetry, for he has used symbols. The word "symbol" in this case, however, has a much wider meaning than it usually has. Symbols are used in all poetry and in much prose, so we must see just what the Symbolist means when he uses the word. Perhaps the best definition is that he seeks ways of symbolizing his feelings.

He may use specific objects which have particular connotations for him, or which may become general rather than personal symbols. Darío's swan, for example, was really a symbol of the Parnassian objective; the swan was an ideal of beauty, a beauty which was above all other things and qualities. The symbol of the swan as an identification of the Modernist's search for beauty became so general that some years later, when the Mexican, Enrique González Martínez, wrote another poetic manifesto calling for a more profound poetry, he entitled the poem, "Wring the Neck of the Swan." If he had been writing only of Darío, he might have substituted "Princess" for "Swan" (See "Sonatina").

He may also make use of color. The color blue became as much a symbol of Modernism as the grace of the swan. Blue also was the unattainable, the artistic, the purely aesthetic. Not only blue, but all colors are used as a means of communicating impressions. The enchantment of Darío's "Sonatina" is to a large extent the result of the richness and variety of color used. Gutiérrez Nájera carries the use of color or the lack of it to an extreme in his poem "Whiteness."

The same poem will also serve as an example of the use of rhythm in an attempt to gain an effect. The effect is rather monotonous in this particular poem, but a more varied and better use of rhythm may be noted in Silva's "Nocturne." Music was a tool of the Symbolists, not only as it was created through the rhythm of the verse, but for the purpose of direct association. Gutiérrez Nájera, for example, wrote a poem called "Schubert's Serenade" in which he attempts to create through poetry the feeling of the music. Gautier, the Parnassian, wrote a "Symphony in White Major"; Rubén Darío wrote a "Symphony in Gray Minor." Rimbaud, an associate of Verlaine, wrote "A Sonnet of Vowels" in which he identified each vowel by color. These sounds and colors were used in the hope that they would evoke reactions in the reader similar to the reactions in the poet, and that the reader, by granting his imagination liberty, would allow the suggestion to extend itself beyond the limits of primary suggestion. So it is that Julio Herrera y Reissig in writing of an unrequited and frustrating love speaks of "the gray sarcasm of her glove" and "the red of my jealousy."

Herrera's use of color as a description of a noun which would not normally take a color-adjective is using another of the most common Symbolist techniques which the Spanish-American Modernists adopted, that is an extraordinary and unexpected association of words which tends to shock the reader into an impression which is beyond the commonplace. The association might be a rather simple one, as with the color association, or it might be far more suggestive as in the same poet's use in "July" of "eucharistic flock." The association might involve a more extensive figure like "when fantastical fireflies were shedding their glow in the damp nuptial shadow" from Silva's "Nocturne" or Lugones' "lunar tranquillity of luminous silk" from "The White Solitude." This line from Lugones shows also how the Symbolist would strive for effect by use of particular vocal sounds in alliteration or in extraordinarily frequent use of the same sound. Silva's "Nocturne" is one of the best examples of this technique.

The Symbolists inherited from Romanticism a love for the exotic, and in many of their works the exotic becomes another symbol of the unattainable, of artistic perfection, and it may be said also that what seems to be occasionally a deliberate vagueness enhances the feeling of a sought-for ideal. In a poem like Darío's "Sonatina" vagueness becomes the very essence of the poem, because "Sonatina" must be understood as the expression of something ethereal, emotional rather than real, made of dreams rather than of material, and of yearning rather than of hope. The road to this kind of expression was not one for a careless poet. If the poet was to cherish any hope of successful communication with the reader, he had to trust the reader and he had also to do everything in his power as a creative writer to inspire his reader into participation. Word choice was therefore of prime importance to the Symbolist and to the Spanish-American Modernist. He had to search for the exact word or what seemed to be the exact word, and sometimes he thought he might enhance his effect by using a word no longer in general use or by using one that never had been in general use.

The Spanish-American Modernists inherited all these techniques and all these attitudes from the French Symbolists. The Americans accepted them but did not follow them as a school. The movement that is called Modernism in Spanish America has characteristics of Symbolism and of Parnassianism and of qualities that are more easily identified with earlier Spanish literature than with either of the two schools of French poetry. The search for words, for instance, led the Spanish-American poets into a verbal over-expression which is reminiscent of the Gongorism of Spain's Golden Age. Like Modernism, Gongorism was an attempt to enrich and to elevate poetry. It was intended to make poetry a special thing belonging to a special group. It was, to be brief, a tendency to make poetry precious. There is extensive use among the Spanish-American Modernists of traditional Spanish verse forms; one in particular, the Argentine, Lugones, wrote a number of *romances* which are inspired by their Spanish predecessors and which indicate also how the Spanish-American Modernist frequently deviated from the Symbolist ideal, because Lugones is more concerned with things as against impressions than is generally the case with the Symbolists. There is evident in some of Lugones' poetry (it may be seen in "The White Solitude" to some extent), a mystic quality which existed in Modernist poetry running along a scale of intensity from frustration of ideals and dissatisfaction with self to the religiosity of Amado Nervo. It is also worth noting that the Modernist poets differed from their Romantic predecessors in that they did not reject the Hispanic tradition. They were influenced by it not only subconsciously but willingly. When they went to Europe, they were as interested in going to Spain as they were in going to France. In other words, the Hispanic tradition was again recognized.

One might well ask how Modernism may be considered a refinement, an extension of Romantic expression, if all of these differences existed in fact. The reason is, of course, that Romantic expression grew toward the motivation that required these techniques. As the Romantic movement grew old, its fire was lost; its impulse to action for personal freedom disappeared and was replaced by exaggerated sentiment and the melancholy of frustration, a frustration which resulted perhaps from the inability to achieve the Romantic ideal of perfect personal freedom. The explosive political situations which had accompanied the intense activity of Romanticism had disappeared and political stability reigned. Writers were therefore in a better position to pursue their aesthetic ideal in all its purity. Much of the excess baggage of Romanticism was eliminated by the Modernists, but the melancholy, the yearning, the self-martyrdom of the Romantics remained. Subjectivism remained, although it was given a new kind of expression. Personalism remained and was intensified, for there is nothing more selfish than the Modernist's tendency not only to write for a select group, but to withdraw himself from the current of everyday affairs into his artificial world of beauty.

2. A Reaction against Realism

While literary growth outward from Romanticism tended in poetry to be in the first place a simplification of expression, the tendency in prose was to substitute for the exaggerated sentimentality of Romanticism, an exquisitely objective view of life. This growth into what is commonly called Realism was so honest, so complete in its portrayal of ordinary life that beauty had to be sought through the commonplace, through the vulgar, and through what many people considered ugly and offensive. Realism in Spanish America was greatly influenced by French Realism, but it was just as clearly a product of Hispanic *costumbrista* literature, a kind of writing which always existed in Spain and which flourished in the nineteenth century with the objective of talking about ordinary life and of pointing out the numerous and relatively unimportant successes and failures of human beings. *Costumbrismo* had never demanded the objectivity that French Realism demanded. Later, this disciplinary objectivity was reinforced by the damning fatalism of Naturalism. Not even prose could incorporate the utter hopelessness of Naturalism in Spanish America or in Spain, because such an attitude was too directly opposed to the traditional religion of the people. Poetry had long since declared itself in reaction against even the relatively mild objectivity and vulgarity of Realism.

The Modernist reaction against Realism was a declaration of the necessity for the search for beauty. By beauty the Modernist meant not the beauty of human reactions as might be witnessed in Realistic prose, nor even beauty of any particular object for its own sake, but rather a beauty for beauty's sake. Parnassianism and Symbolism had become art for art's sake, and so Modernism was to a large extent that sort of thing. It is this search for beauty that best expresses the Modernist's frustration and affords the best reason for his melancholy. Beauty became an indefinable something, a mystic power, an unattainable god. Various symbols were used for its description: the color was blue, the figure was the swan. These two symbols were common to all Modernists. Personal symbols were developed by the various poets, and a few of them grew beyond purely personal expression. It should be quite clear that if this beauty which was being sought had been attainable, it would not have achieved its purpose, for the Modernist poet felt the need of facing the unattainable, of knowing that he could never satisfy the longing that he felt. Such a mystic pursuit of an abstract beauty enabled the poet to withdraw from the world around him, to reject his obligations to public affairs, and to confine himself more and more to a select group of writers and readers. Few people would care to deny the right of poets to refuse to identify themselves with the taste of the mass of people. Even fewer would deny that the poet must struggle against the tendency to write only for himself. It was easy for the Modernist poets to feel sorry for themselves. They could support their feelings by reference to their French contemporaries and especially by reference to the father of modern Romance poetry, Charles Baudelaire. Baudelaire in his masterful comparison of the poet and the albatross had said: "exiled on earth in the midst of hooting crowds, his great wings hinder him when he tries to walk." The Modernists accepted their martyrdom with great joy, just as the Romantics had wallowed in their excessive grief.

Since the Modernist poet felt under no obligation to address the general public, he was free to do very nearly anything he wished to do; and since what he wished to do most of all was to identify himself with an unattainable abstract beauty, with an exquisite delicacy, with a fragile loveliness, his poetry became quite precious. Let us take Darío's "Sonatina" as an example. It carries no message, it communicates an illusion. It is a successful poem because it does just that. Although Darío mentions specific, tangible things, these things do not together form a material reality. Rather, the interplay of colors, of mounting sadness, of ennui, of feigned gaiety, of immense wealth, and of infinite luxury, form not a picture but a kaleidoscope of emotional reactions. "Sonatina" is a china teacup, but it is more than that; it is enough in variety to remove the poet and the sympathetic reader entirely from the material world. In this particular poem, the excellence of the verse contributes a great deal to the total effect.

The search for abstract beauty led Modernist poets in several different directions. Darío in "Sonatina" took the road of wealth and marble palaces and nobility. His attitude amounts to a love of legendary grandeur. Other poets took the road of geographical distance. Julián del Casal sought beauty in things of the Orient; Ricardo Jaimes Freyre sought it in the unfamiliar lands of snow and wolves and sleighs ("The Sad Voices"); Amado Nervo sought it through religious mysticism. All these poets sought essentially the same thing. They chose these several ways as steps toward the unattainable beauty of which they had dreamed. It is not likely that any of these poets really believed that he was progressing very far toward his ideal of beauty; he must have recognized that the unfamiliar territory into which he reached was removed from his own world only by his lack of knowledge of it and did not represent a genuine step toward the ideal. The actual step toward the ideal was to be found in the effect of the poet's creative effort, and here the vagueness and the charming delicacy of "Sonatina" will serve as evidence of what the Modernists meant to contribute toward the search for beauty.

Late in the Golden Age of Spanish literature, Luis de Góngora became the high priest of a school of poetry which took his name (Gongorism) and which was similar to Marinism in Italy, Preciosité in France, and Euphuism in England. In many ways the Modernist movement in Spanish America was a sort of neo-Gongorism. Most of the Modernist poets showed great interest in Spanish poetry and Luis de Góngora was not the least of their interests. For poets who were inclined to make a rather personal and obscure thing of their art, the involved conceits of Gongorism were a source of endless enchantment. There is no question that the Modernists profited from their attention to Góngora and that Spanish-American poetry profited from their attention to peninsular poetry in general. Their study served to renew a tradition which had always existed, but which for some years had suffered neglect. The reading of Góngora strengthened their tendency to seek the precise word needed for the expression of what they wished to say, and it encouraged them toward enriching their expression by the use of uncommon words. Such poetic activity can admittedly become extremely silly, but its influence on the tradition of writing poetry in a given place depends upon the motivation more than on the immediate result. It might be fair to say that the literary evils resulting from exaggerated Gongorism in Spain were the product of an overly refined society which then found itself approaching the precipice. Such a society was incapable of expressing itself in bold terms and intellectuality took refuge in the obtuse. Such was not the case in Spanish America, because Modernism marks the beginning of Spanish America's most productive literary period. Its preciousness existed, perhaps, because for the first time in the national history of Spanish America the political situation was sufficiently stable to allow writers to turn from the necessities of the moment and to create their paths, reaching toward an abstract beauty. There is an interesting contradiction in this process, for the Modernist movement was at once a withdrawal from reality and a definite step toward the intellectual independence of Hispanic America. It was the most creative body of literature that Spanish America had produced up to that time. In spite of various influences it was a movement with its own identity. and yet it really did not propose to be either national or even American in quality; and the truth is that if we generalize, it was neither of these things. Many of the best poets of Modernism could hardly be claimed by any particular country. Darío, principal figure of the movement, is as much the poet of the whole continent as a man could be, and, still, although he belonged to the whole continent, he is not the poet of Spanish America. He is really the American poet of western civilization. It is true that in some of his later poems his feelings may be identified with certain things that are characteristically American, but in general he was removed from such easy recognition. The question remains, however, as to why Darío or any other Modernist poet ever descended from his ivory tower in order to identify himself with place and problems. The probable answer is that, since Modernism came at a time when Spanish America was achieving intellectual independence, even the isolationist tendency of Modernists had to be influenced by the current introspective activity. With Realism, the Spanish Americans had looked at themselves more carefully than they ever had before and they began to discover and to understand a number of the social problems that existed in their countries.

3. A Coming of Age in Spanish-American Poetry

After the years of imitation and anarchy in Spanish America, it is natural to expect some indications of increasing maturity. The creative work of the Modernist poets is one aspect of intellectual independence which is complemented by realistic consideration of social conditions in the Spanish-American countries. In another genre, the essay, Spanish-American writers considered not only social conditions within their particular countries or in Spanish America as a whole, but also considered the position of Spanish America and of the individual countries in western civilization. Much thought was given to what might be considered the proper background of Spanish America, whether the background was Hispanic or Latin or European or American. As a matter of fact, the background was all of these things, but the point for consideration was how these backgrounds should be regarded in the search for an expression and in the search for a national philosophy. To phrase it another way, it seemed to many Spanish-American thinkers that Spanish-American national efforts needed to be based on the existing tradition and they wished to define that tradition. All three of these considerations then—the position in western civilization of the Spanish-American nations, the internal social and political problems of those nations, and the purely artistic production of those nations—were expressions of cultures that had reached an age of self-determination. For the first time, the writers of the Spanish-American nations were oriented toward independence.

The genuine consciousness of Spanish America's peculiar situation came as a result of time for contemplation. There is no doubt that the Romantic tendency toward intense activity combined with the confusion and doubt in the lives of the young Spanish-American republics, had created an atmosphere which did not lead men to contemplation, nor to the consciousness of the fact that time was available for introspective consideration. During the early years of the republics, interpretations of "Americanism" were superficial and it was only toward the end of the nineteenth century that the word was interpreted with greater depth of meaning. It was, of course, toward the end of the nineteenth century that the political situation in Spanish America became relatively stable, particularly in the countries where the greatest amount of literary production was to be expected and, although this stability may not always have been of the most desirable sort, as witness the Díaz regime in Mexico, it was nevertheless the cause of a sufficient amount of calm to allow the writers to turn their attention to their tasks as writers rather than to encourage them to express themselves in a frenzy typical of the exterior world.

The self-examination that was encouraged by Realism in the novel led into the contemporary novel of social protest. During the last years of the nineteenth century, Spanish Americans finally saw and confessed to the mistreatment of the Indian, and the problem was attacked in fiction and in essay. There was also some indication of recognition of the rural-urban conflict. The Modernist poets tended toward a sort of conservatism which did not allow them to deal with the ugly aspects of life that were appearing in fiction and in essay. Their conservatism was not genuinely political, but was rather a lack of willingness to sacrifice this opportunity for purely artistic expression to the demands of social protest. They were not ready for a period of social upheaval, so they retreated from the protest and reflected the exterior calm of their times by divorcing themselves from human problems and seeking refuge in the beautiful.

It must be remembered, however, that just as exterior calm is characteristic of the times, so was the growing consciousness of America and of various nationalities. And so we find during the course of Modernism in poetry a tendency both general and individual toward a recognition of the real situation and away from the ivory tower. Rubén Darío descended from the heights of "Sonatina" and wrote an extremely declamatory poem to Theodore Roosevelt showing his hate and his pride and his fear, these things being Hispanic-American qualities rather than his individual ones. Lugones in Argentina became more and more conscious of the tremendous significance of the gaucho in Argentine culture, and José Santos Chocano in Peru wrote the group of poems from which "Who Knows?" is taken and which attempts to show the qualities of the Indian that had placed him in his particular social situation. It would be wrong, however, to say that social comment was an important part of Modernist poetry. The Americanism which came from Modernist poetic expression resides in the independence of creative effort. The actual social comment is indicative of a kind of poetry that was to come in a later period.

THE TRAJECTORY OF MODERNIST POETRY

The second generation of Romantic poets had spent themselves by the mid-eighties and literary history from that time becomes concerned with the development of Modernism. The poets who are generally referred to as the precursors of Modernism are hardly precursors in a chronological sense, since the publication of Rubén Darío's *Azure* (1888) was as early as the work of any of the so-called precursors, and the same author's *Lay Hymns*, which may be regarded as the apogee of Modernism, was published in 1896, only a year or two after the works of the precursors. The precursors, then, were really contemporaries of the full-fledged Modernists and rather than genuine precursors were semi-Modernists. The four poets, Gutiérrez Nájera, Martí, Casal, and Silva, were all identified in one way or another with the characteristics that were Modernist, but none of them was as fully devoted to beauty for its own sake as the genuine Modernist was. Gutiérrez Nájera in 1887 wrote his "When I Die" with a great economy of expression if not of sentiment. The hope of the overwrought poet is good evidence of the kinship between the frustration of the Romantic and the frustration of the Modernist. "Whiteness," which was written in 1888, was closer to real Modernism because of its combined emphasis on rhythm, color, and feeling. Much of the earlier Modernist poetry, including Darío's first volume, is closer to Parnassianism than to Symbolism. The two influences were mixed, the tendency being to progress from Parnassian to Symbolist influence. Silva's "Nocturne" is an attempt at subjective communication while his "Art" is more Parnassian. He is more concerned with the beauty of form in this particular poem than with communicating an impression. The idea that he communicates is applicable to his more Symbolistic poetry. The communication of impression is important to Silva because much of his poetry is the product of a desperate sadness. Here a Romantic inclination was enhanced by the tragic circumstances of his life, and it is a tribute to the new attitude toward poetry that the author's melancholy did not completely dominate his art. Fortunately, Silva was able to establish a communication which creates sympathy and understanding on the part of his reader as well as delight in the sheer beauty of some of his expression. With the exception of a few occasions when Silva's poetry becomes embittered, he concerns himself with the expression of a very delicate sort of love, seeking to find general qualities that would apply to all kinds of love at their best. Being unable to state this feeling as a fact, Silva relied to a large extent on the creation of an impression and in general cared relatively little for form.

Much of the same melancholy can be found in the poems of Gutiérrez Nájera and Casal. There is a tendency to cherish sadness and one cannot help feeling that this very sadness which the poets were grasping was in some way an expression of the ideal they sought. Perhaps the sadness they express was not really sadness, but only a word or an idea, maybe the best they could find to express the longing which was within them. Perhaps this longing was for the unattainable something which we have called abstract beauty. It is interesting, however, that Casal, certainly one of the most pessimistic of poets, notes a difference between his own outlook and that of Darío when the latter was passing through Cuba in 1892. In his "Pages of Life" the words are supposed to be those of Darío, except the last two stanzas which are Casal's own commentary. One would expect from this poem that Darío is a great deal more optimistic than Casal; and such was probably the case in 1892, but the rosy hue of that year faded from the view of the poet who later said that "Nothing gives more pain than just to be alive can give." Some twelve years had passed since Darío had talked with Casal and the brilliant surface of Modernist delicacy was beginning to shatter.

Perhaps it is the nature of movements that seek unattainable ideals to rise momentarily to a peak of brilliance and then become diluted. Such had been the course of Romanticism, if Romanticism be interpreted in the strictest sense of the course of the Romantic Movement. Now again in Modernism another expression of romantic feelings and unattainable ideals had gradually developed into the infinitely beautiful expression of purest Modernism only to have the undeniable fact of life start the diluting process immediately. To a large extent the history of the Modernist movement may be seen in the works of Rubén Darío. Darío's first poems were written in the fading Romantic tradition, but his attitudes were clearly tending toward a variation and the variation which we call Modernism was definitively begun with the publication of *Azure* in 1888. Darío claimed that he was unfamiliar with Hugo's statement that art is blue, but that blue for him meant beauty and dreams. In *Azure* he attempts to express himself by devotion to beauty of form, by cultivation of a vagueness of expression, and by suggestion of disillusionment on account of his not belonging to his time and place, and by his inability to reach another world. Darío comes closest to reaching that other world in *Lay Hymns* which was published in 1896. This volume may well mark the highest point of Modernist poetry, and more than any other volume it incorporates the purest escape from earthly vulgarity. "The Swan" and "Sonatina" together form the keynote of the book. There may well be biographical factors which created in Darío a sensuous love of luxury. Certainly in his poetry it becomes a symbol of his ideal. The swan also expresses this ideal, and identifies the ideal as something new, something different. *Lay Hymns* reveals to us a man steeped in the literature of France and of Spain, in the Classics, and particularly in mythology. It reveals to us a man who by his artistic taste cannot cause himself to fit into the world in which he was born. To what extent this dilemma was an individual problem and to what extent it was characteristic of Darío's time we cannot say. We know only that before Darío, the artist, was able to face the world in which he lived or even to face himself, he first found it necessary to retreat completely from reality and build himself a world of vague dreams, of clouded beauty, of feigned animation, and of joy or sorrow which were in no way the product of an intellectual process. At first glance, the *Lay Hymns* may seem superficial. They are not. Their depth, however, is emotional; they carry no profound philosophical message. They carry no direct message at all. Rather, they carry a message that needs to be felt, that needs to be suggested by the clouds and sounds and colors and illusions and shapes and feelings and associations of which Darío writes. To be accepted at all, they must be accepted on this emotional level, not on the level of wondering what concise message the poet is elaborating in his verses. The year 1896 and the ensuing three or four years mark the peak of Modernism not only for Darío, but for the movement in general. The road of retreat from reality was a temporary one, which in most cases—and certainly in the case of Darío—prepared the poet to come down from his ivory tower, and intellectualize his reactions toward life. In *Songs of Life and of Hope* which was published in 1905, Darío is no longer the expectant wanderer in marble palaces. He has gained confidence in himself, gained assurance regarding the legitimacy of the poet's position in the world, and gained respect for the Hispanic heritage. Rubén Darío was a great poet and so his changing point of view did not cause him in any way to reject the influences that had formed him as an artist, but rather to mold those influences to his needs at that time. The poet's descent into the world of reality does not mean that he deserted his quest for the beautiful, nor that he gave up the use of delicate expression in his poetry. It does mean that he was ready to use all his poetic sensitivity in a consideration of himself in his world. He felt that he was no longer young; and the search for his ideal took a rather different route. Perhaps he realizes that the ideal is unattainable; but, if he does know this, he knows also that it has to be unattainable. Pessimism in Darío is accepted without bitterness, without ire. By 1907 when Darío published *The Errant Song,* the Modernist cycle was about complete. The master had reached the point not only of viewing himself in the world, not only of revealing and contemplating his likes and dislikes and his hopes and his fears, but even of expressing himself violently in a poem written against Theodore Roosevelt. His specific expression of America is limited to patriotic ideas. Many poets, some even among the Modernists, made far greater use of American themes. Darío was a cosmopolitan poet, and it was this very cosmopolitanism that made him most American in that he did what was most necessary in his time. He led Spanish-American poetry through a path that it needed very much to follow: of rejection of the material world in order that its aesthetic principles might become established and gain strength, and then back from the ivory tower to the introspection that was needed, allied with the strengthened artistic tradition. By 1910 Modernism had largely run its course. The Modernist poets in general were coming down from the ivory tower. It was in 1911 that Enríque González Martínez demanded that the swan's neck be twisted and that the graceful but intellectually inadequate swan be replaced by the more thoughtful owl.

The Modernist poets achieved their escape through different routes as may be seen in this volume. Ricardo Jaimes Freyre, in his *Pagan Fount* managed to create for himself and to some extent for his readers a classical land with Nordic overtones, the effect of which was to create in the reader a feeling of non-reality, and of pursuing a happiness which is constantly almost within grasp, but which constantly slips just a little farther away. Amado Nervo followed the very different path of religious mysticism. The names of some of his volumes indicate his road: *Serenity, Elevation, Plenitude.*

A large part of Nervo's poetry was written after the course of Modernism had turned toward the descent from the ivory tower. In his particular case the descent had little meaning because his own expression followed a religious development rather than a purely aesthetic one. Among his earliest poems is one to Thomas á Kempis in which he writes of his consuming interest in the religious. Occasionally Nervo departed from the primarily religious, but always there are overtones of his faith. A volume called *The Constant Beloved* would fall within this description and has furnished the poem "Why Weep? No More!" for this anthology. Nervo's religious feeling progressed through a kind of pantheism to a resignation which sometimes seems more Buddhist than Christian. When he deals with human problems in his poetry, he is inclined to over-simplify the case, and the reader sometimes feels that the poet is doggedly insisting that everything will be all right. There is a deceptiveness in Nervo's poetry which comes from his ability to make his idea sound as if it were the answer to a great problem. This he does in "If You Are Good." But after reading it and considering it, one must admit that the author really hasn't said very much after all. "Fill It With Love" is another case of the same thing. From the standpoint of communication of enduring feeling, "Solidarity" is a better poem than either of these two. This is true, perhaps, because it carries no stated message, and because its feeling of happiness and kinship with all things is something that many people would like to accept. "Solidarity" preceded both "If You Are Good" and "Fill It With Love." It belongs to the volume *Serenity*. "If You Are Good" is from *Elevation* and "Fill It With Love" is found in *Plenitude*. The three poems are very good examples of three progressive stages in Nervo's thinking. In the last stage, he had virtually deserted poetry and was writing prose in his attempt to add emphasis to the idea.

Nervo's position in literature is a peculiar one and suggests some ideas as to the contemporary reception of Modernist expression. Like all his contemporaries, Nervo was considered a bit odd in his time. But since then, he has come to be perhaps the most popular of the Modernist poets. He is read widely and to a great extent because he says what people think they wish to believe. He says comforting things. He promises the reader that if he is good—and, of course, everybody wishes to be good—he will know everything. He tells the reader that if the reader has any problems to solve, all he has to do is love a lot, and the problems will disappear. No one would wish to object to these feelings, but if Nervo is going to be read only for these reasons he must be considered inadequate as a poet, for he has said things that are comforting rather than helpful and he has pleased his reader by giving him a sugar-coated pill rather than by demanding something on the part of the reader. Present day critics are inclined to accuse Nervo of this inadequacy and to find his poetry trite. It is necessary to state also that present day criticism must find fault with some of the works of practically all of the Modernists, because the gaily dressed princesses and the pastel palaces of ivory tower expression have become a little tired. Much of the same has happened as happened in the case of Romanticism: the exaggeration of Romantic expression became tiresome and only when Romantic expression was at its best is it really acceptable in our time. Similarly the dream world of the Modernist may seem completely ridiculous to the reader of our time. The exaggerated escape of the Modernist is as apt to produce a chuckle in the present day reader as is the fainting hero of Romanticism. The most durable expression of the Modernists came after their aesthetic purification when they allowed themselves to come down and live among ordinary men.

Very early in the writings of Leopoldo Lugones there appeared two developments away from what Modernism was at its peak. One of these tendencies was to allow himself such freedom in the creation of images by extraordinary and vague association that his poetry became very difficult to understand; and the other tendency was to deal with material things surrounding him rather than seek the marble palaces of Modernist imagination. Lugones was enough of a poet to combine these two things, and he has had an occasional successor in the post-Modernist period.

Among the poets who are generally considered Modernists proper, there are two in whose work the two deviations in the work of Lugones become characteristic. José Santos Chocano had from the beginning emphasized American themes. Principally, what he did was declare the duality of his Indian-Spanish background in his manifesto and proceed to pay a great deal of attention to things of nature that were typically American, and to distinctions in the American people. The latter meant a consideration of the Indian character. In poems like his "Who Knows?" Chocano expressed very well the Indian characteristics which appear enigmatic to the white man. In this particular poem and in some others, the poet's artistic capacity sustains the beauty of the poem along with the social expression. In some other poetry of Chocano, poetic beauty is sacrificed to the expression of idea.

The other path of Modernism is exemplified in the poems of Julio Herrera y Reissig. His use of symbols often not made clear to the reader makes his poetry very difficult, and it is only after repeated readings that the sequence of symbols becomes a pattern of emotional responses. Such a response is too vague to lend itself to interpretation of the poem. What happens in a poem like "July" is that the reader goes through a series of sensory reactions, of sickness, of fear, of strangeness, of feeling apart from the world, of loneliness, of discomfort before the past, of a needed thanksgiving accompanied by a reluctance to express it, and of a fear that the world is something forbidding because it is totally beyond the comprehension of the poet. These are some of the reactions of "July." The emotional pattern created in the reader must of necessity depend upon his own experience. The reader actually becomes an important part of the creative act.

Both Chocano and Herrera y Reissig indicate two paths which poetry subsequent to Modernism would take. When, in 1911, González Martínez demanded that the swan's neck be twisted, he was not referring either to Chocano or Herrera. He certainly understood that Chocano had come out from the marble palace, and he must have understood also that Herrera's impressions were the product not so much of an escape from reality as the expression of a super-reality in which the impression was not a spontaneous emotional one, but one that had passed through an intellectual process. González Martínez is really the last of the Modernists. He called for the change and he progressed out of the retreat and fully into the realization of life. His poetry becomes profound, his expression as such becomes clear, though his ideas are sometimes difficult. Perhaps his finest expression is that of a feeling which most people have had, the inability to go back. This he expresses with consummate grace in "An Impossible Return." There could be no more convincing example than the poetry of González Martínez himself of the salutary influence of the Modernist aesthetic retreat, for his poetry, which is conceived well within the actual world, benefits immeasurably from the influence of the quest for beauty.

POETRY SINCE MODERNISM

The changed perspective created by the passing of many years will probably show us that there is no real division between the period called Modernist and the later poetry which has sometimes been called post-Modernism. As we look at the two periods now, the only real difference evident is the Modernist's retreat into the ivory tower. After this retreat had served its purpose, even those poets who are called Modernists proper were able to come down from the tower and see themselves in a more realistic world. Among the Modernists, we have also seen the starting points of two tendencies which were to be the two general characteristics of post-Modernist poetry: (1) the tendency toward a consistently more obscure and less understandable expression and (2) the recognition and use of material things surrounding the poet. We might create an imaginary scale at one end of which would be the poets who stated very simply their reaction to the social environment in which they found themselves and at the other end of which we would find the Surrealist poets. Along the scale we would find the poets who were less concerned with an expression of the social environment than of certain personal reactions to life within that environment, all this expressed quite simply and obviously. Continuing along the scale we would find that some of this personal expression used symbols and references which are not always understood by the reader and which therefore make the poetry less comprehensible. Remove this tendency from personal experience, and apply personal symbols to exterior matters, and we find the poetry still more difficult, though entirely comprehensible with study and consideration. And finally at the last point of the scale would be the Surrealists whose poetry has no apparent meaning at all, but rather appears to be a jumble of startling words, symbols and phrases.

It is impossible to make any reasonable classification of the poets since Modernism. Some artificial classifications can be made which might help a student memorize the material. We might establish a category of poets of personal experience, or of poets who love mankind, or of poets who question the fundamental honesty of man, or of poets of Nature, or of satirical poets, or of women poets. None of these classifications is valid because each represents an attempt to consider only one aspect of each poet. One of the favorite classifications has been the women poets. There are four very eminent women poets of the period since Modernism: Delmira Agustini, Alfonsina Storni, Juana de Ibarbourou, and Gabriela Mistral. These poets are treated time after time as a unit of study because they are women. While it is true that their poetry bears certain characteristics in common because they are all women, the classification is not valid from a poetic point of view. Possibly it might be valid from a sociological point of view, because all four of the women write of their love for men and either talk about or imply feelings arising from their maternal instinct. It is hardly surprising that a woman poet should do so, but there is little point in considering her in a classification different from the man who writes purely personal poetry. It will be seen as a matter of fact that the work of each of these women poets possesses certain qualities which place it in closer relationship with some of the other poetry of the time than with the poetry of the rest of the women. So it is better to avoid classification. If we visualize our imaginary scale, any of the poets of the period might be placed in more than one position on the scale, and, if we were to study the change in the works of all the poets of the period in an attempt to arrive at some generalization of tendencies, we should probably find that there is a tendency toward a position on the scale which is short of the Surrealistic, but which represents the position of a kind of poetry which is decidedly obscure and which demands a very considerable contribution on the part of the reader. The most extreme sort of poetic expression has often received praise for having enriched poetry by introducing new figures, and new concepts, and by providing a certain freedom of expression which is salutary. Not very much attention has been given the motivation of the extreme poetry and how this motivation has influenced the general tendency toward a poetry not quite so extreme but still rather obscure.

The extreme or experimental poetry has its roots in Modernism itself, particularly in the poetry of Herrera y Reissig, but it should be made quite clear that Herrera's poetry is only a starting point. During the twenties there were a number of names invented for avant-garde poetry and a number of manifestoes issued with regard to it. The most widely used name was Ultraism, which implies that the poets intended to go beyond Modernism. Many people have felt that they meant to go beyond in the extreme use of language, but the general intent was to go beyond Modernism in an intellectual sense.

Ultraism was a more generally used term than was Creationism in Chile or Stridentism in Mexico. These two terms applied to specific groups of poets who declared their intentions and proceeded for a short while to put them into effect. The poets generally outgrew the manifesto and the small groups never produced a poet of great stature who worked within the framework of the manifesto. Still the small groups may show best of all what the motivation of avant-garde poetry was and this is important because a modification of this motivation is the source of much contemporary poetic expression in Spanish America. Perhaps the most eminent combination of school and man is Vicente Huidobro and Chilean Creationism. Huidobro believed that a creative act took place in the poetic selection of words and in the placing of words on paper. Something new was born, something that had far more significance than the literal meaning of the words, and in order to complete this creative act, the reader himself had to perform a creative act which consisted of leaving himself completely open to the suggestion of what the poet was saying—not open in a passive way, but open to suggestion and willing to work with it and let the suggestion act within the reader's own consciousness and subconsciousness toward the formation of creative response on the part of the reader. If the reader expects the poem to communicate an idea to him immediately, Huidobro's verses will seem the work of a mad man, and even people who have done a great deal toward making Huidobro's poetry understood, have wondered at times if he were pulling their leg. He was not. Huidobro and the poets in whom we find a similar motivation may fail sometimes in their efforts, but they are not guilty of deceit. Theirs is a quest for the expression of reality. The reality which they are looking for is an interior reality; not an exterior one. One kind of reality is exterior, visual reality: things that can be seen or even emotions or results of emotions that can be evaluated objectively. These things lend themselves to direct description in poetry and, used in various associations, they can be made a rich experience. The Modernist poet sought and expressed another kind of reality which may be called emotional reality. That is to say, he intended to express not a thought but a feeling, a feeling which was communicable by creating certain impressions which he had received at a given moment on a given occasion. The Ultraist poets or the Creationists or whatever poets of the avant-garde—they all have the same motivation fundamentally—sought a still different reality which was the reality of the subconscious. The poet sought to express and to communicate the feeling which was within himself, not the feeling which he experienced as the result of the impression of a given moment, but the feeling that was the result of many impressions which had been felt, then intellectualized, then made a part of himself. This reality he saw as the motivation of his actions, and this reality he therefore regarded as the most genuine of all the views of reality. There is no doubt that expression of this reality is an extremely difficult task and it has been best done by those poets like Jorge Luis Borges and Torres Bodet and López Velarde and Pablo Neruda, who have been able to use it within the framework of material, visual reality.

Delmira Agustini is perhaps the closest to genuine Modernism of all the poets usually assigned to the post-Modernist trends. Her first volume of poetry was published in 1907, only two years after the publication of Darío's *Songs of Life and of Hope*. Her chronological position combined with the egocentricity of her expression to lead her along the road of Modernism. While the lyric quality of Agustini's poetry is undeniable, it must be admitted that her expression is very narrow as to subject matter. All of her poems are the product of her own frustrated love. In all fairness to the poet, it should be noted that these verses are the expression of a very youthful person who had hardly had time to develop a breadth of vision even if she had the ability. Agustini's poems have the disadvantage of losing identification with the reader, who is inclined to interest himself in what the poems reveal of Agustini's life, rather than allow his own poetic being to communicate with her. Certainly one would not find fault with the poetry as artistic expression. One might very well find fault with the intensely personal quality of it. Enrique Banchs and Rafael Alberto Arrieta are also extremely personal in their expression. These two poets are much more inclined to speak of the ordinary things surrounding them than Modernists were, but their manner of expression is essentially the same no matter how familiar the things treated may be. They are handled with the same delicacy and with the same lack of probing. Banchs' poem, "The Tiger," is a magnificent use of words to describe an emotion. It is, however, nothing more than a single sustained figure, and the description is of a generalized emotion which lacks the specific strength and power of communication of a particular case. Even if the reader should never have experienced a particular case, just the same he is more apt to understand and identify with the particular case than he is with a generalization. The generalization is always registered as such and is regarded as impersonal by the reader. In other poems, Banchs shows a similar ability for handling words, but rarely are his emotions very profound and rarely does he succeed in commanding the identification of his reader. Of all the poems it is only in "The Vow" that Banchs has linked himself through a fine expression of his own humility with a feeling probably familiar to most of his readers. Certainly every person who has honestly felt the desire to sing of what he felt will be able to understand the feeling of the artist in "The Vow." Arrieta is more attracted by the things about him than is Banchs; but as can be noted in "In an Abandoned Cemetery" he is inclined to focus all these things toward himself and his private world. It should not be understood that there is anything wrong about doing this, nor even unusual. Quite to the contrary, it is very natural for the poet to center himself among these surrounding things; but although, in the work of some other poets, the person of the poet may be the center of the surrounding things, the things may not exist quite so much for the sake of the person.

Alfonsina Storni is concerned not only with surrounding things, but with surrounding circumstances. Far from the wide-eyed disillusionment of Delmira Agustini, Storni is the essence of bitterness that comes from complete frustration, rather than amatory disillusionment. Storni wants love, but she also wants freedom from love and freedom to love and yet she hates her position in society as a woman. She resents the burden that women must carry in order to fulfill the role she accords them as the very foundation of the social order. She is disgusted with the smallness of men and of their pretenses as regards women; and seeing the disposition of women and the presumptuousness of men as the motivating factors in our social order, Alfonsina Storni is disgusted with life and is particularly disgusted with the burden that she is expected to bear. Her irritability reaches the point of making her dissatisfied with everything, and the whole aspect of the material world irritates her more and more so that she is capable of an expression like "Squares and Angles," which in spite of its apparently gay cleverness is the tragic expression of a tragic life. Alfonsina's expression is among the simplest in the Spanish language. It is simple and pure and direct and, at the same time, full enough in concept to be suggestive to the reader. Her verse is generally rhythmic and only rarely does she fall into the sin of shallow rhythm as she does in "Pain." So she is a very unusual combination of elegant expression and violently conceived ideas.

Quite the reverse of Alfonsina is Juana de Ibarbourou. Her poetry is the expression of a woman who has been completely happy in the conventional sense of the word. Her enjoyment of life has been, as a matter of fact, so complete that it is a little humorous to hear her say that she deeply regrets her femininity. Her longing is not for something she would be able to do if she were a man. Rather it is the yearning for more life than is available, for a yet more exquisite happiness. And so, whatever sadness she has comes from joy, and her anxiety to increase the fullness of her life makes her a little pagan in her lack of resignation. Hers is a vivid world. A world in which death is a suggestion, but not a reality. She cannot reconcile herself to the possibility of not living on this earth. As in the case of Storni, her consciousness of things involves other people around her. Her life is controlled by the circumstances of the world in which she lives.

There is a strange similarity between the attitudes of these two women and that of Rafael Arévalo Martínez in their common tendency to concern themselves intimately with the things around them. In the poetry of Arévalo, the character of society becomes an even more important factor. While it cannot be denied that Arévalo has a healthy concern for himself, that concern is primarily in relationship to other men. His feelings toward his fellow humans are wonderfully comprehending of their qualities. Arévalo understands the dignity of each man and the worth of self; and somewhere in his formation as a thinker, he was given an extraordinary ability to discern and express the motivations of himself and his fellows. One of his most interesting ways of expressing these motivations was by comparison of men with different kinds of animals. Happily, the procedure does not become ludicrous, but is beautiful because Arévalo's comparison of men with animals amounts to a statement of fundamental human qualities and, although it may seem at first glance that the poet does not distinguish carefully enough between animals and men, it becomes increasingly apparent that the comparisons really form the basis for contrast. Certainly what Arévalo wishes most of all is an understanding by men of each other and an understanding of themselves to the extent that they may give all of themselves to their living among other men. Arévalo talks mainly in terms of relationships among men, but there is implicit in all his poetry a faith in God who is the ultimate reason for all that the poet wishes.

Up to the present point of progression on our scale, Arévalo is by all odds the poet who feels himself most definitely within society. At about the same point on the scale, Gabriela Mistral, another great poetess, should appear. Her work shows a combined concern for her own salvation, for the expression of her own self, and for the good of her fellow men. But in none of these poets, in spite of their functioning within worldly reality, do we have any specific identification with place. The Mexican López Velarde, perhaps focuses surrounding things more toward himself than Arévalo did, but the scene is more clearly identified. López Velarde is to a large extent a regionalistic poet. When he progressed beyond regionalism he became national. He felt keenly the identification of man with place, his sense of belonging to a series of places growing in size from the town of one's birth or even the house of one's birth to the nation and perhaps even to a larger unit than that. It is interesting to compare López Velarde's poem with González Martínez' "An Impossible Return." López Velarde does return physically but, just as González Martínez had said, he cannot return completely. He cannot return because the place to which he must return is no longer there. It has been changed into something else by the passage of time and of time's allies. It has been marked by battle; and the poet knows that the hopes for which he had returned are destroyed. In this poem we may see a clear development away from what we have been calling Modernism. Every figure that is used to develop a feeling has been intellectualized. When "at the well-curb the leather bucket drips categorically a drop," we know that López Velarde is not trying to create the impression of a moment, but is giving us the result of much thought about his experience, and is hopeful that we will live with this figure, both feeling and intellectualizing until it signifies his own discouragement and lack of hope arising from the refusal of the place which ought to own him, to recognize him as a son. So it is with all his figures, all of them showing that he knows he does not belong, that the place is strange, and that in spite of its commonplace quality, in spite of much that remains of tradition, there is yet a yearning for what *was* rather than for what *is*.

The two poems by Jorge Luis Borges are extraordinarily good examples of his poetic work because they show very well how he excelled in using the things around him in identifying his poetry with his immediate surroundings and was still able to make it a suggestive expression from which the reader could carry on in his own creative participation. The elegance of humble things is seen in "The Patio" and to even a greater extent in "The Guitar." Perhaps it is wrong to see the things mentioned in "The Guitar" as humble things, because the pampa and its inhabitant, the gaucho, represent something of epic quality in Argentina. There has always been an association of the unconquerable with the gaucho and with his pampa. They have been synonymous with freedom and have become the symbol of national liberty. Aside from the eloquence of some of the figures in "The Guitar" the finest thing about the poem is the interpolation of the completely personal note where the poet is reminded of "her" in the midst of all the associations with other things, and then having recognized himself as existing in their midst, the spell is suddenly broken and the guitar stops and the poet is precisely where he was when the spell first began. Borges' poetry reveals an anxiety over the poet's associating himself with his surroundings, which suggests the poet might never be able to express himself completely. It is interesting to note that Borges has stopped writing poetry and has become one of the finest essayists in the Spanish language.

Neither Torres Bodet nor Pablo Neruda may be as closely identified with place as are Borges and López Velarde. They are both, however, very much concerned with material things. Torres Bodet uses material things not only as a means of expressing emotion as he does in this anthology, but also expresses sheer joy in things themselves. Again this is no matter of mere emotion, of mere impression, but is the result of many hours and days and years of mellowing of impression and of choice of suggested images for the communication of an idea. Sometimes the reader feels that Torres Bodet has chosen his figures with too much care, and there is a certain deliberate quality about his poetry which hardens it. There could hardly be a more profound expression of reaction to beautiful sound, however, than is to be found in his poem "Music." This is a feeling that is not to be accepted on the first reading. It is a feeling which must be developed after many, many readings as each figure is lived with and comprehended internally by the reader. Pablo Neruda in "Bridges" has also used material things to express a profound feeling. However, it is in "Barcarolle" that we find his most suggestive poem in this collection. This poem is almost a fear of intimacy. It is a poem of burning desire and reluctance. It is a poem of infinite connotation. What is the sea, and why does the poet speak of weeping by the sea? Is the sea to be associated with the sound of wheels of a sleepy train? What is a sleepy train? Does this express comfort or does it express fear, or simply anticipation of the unknown? These questions cannot and should not be answered definitively, but these are the questions that should come into the mind of the reader. And the chances are good that if the reader lives with the poem long enough and gives enough of himself to the poem, eventually the patterns will form, as the figures of Neruda become figures for the reader. The result will come not only from what the reader feels, but from what the reader has been told, and from what the reader surmises of the reactions of others. The whole reader responds, and so it is that the poet will be understood.

It is likely that some of the Modernists might have felt a little the way Neruda felt when he wrote "Walking Around." They would probably have misunderstood him. They would have thought that he wanted to retreat from a material world. Actually Neruda wishes no such thing. What he is saying is that he is tired of material limitations on things. That a man must always be nothing more than a man is a boring fact. That he must always be tied to that category and must always perform the functions of man is an eminently discouraging fact; and in this particular poem, he offers no hope, except that in the very expression of his dissatisfaction with the material, he has made himself more than just man. And in poems like "Barcarolle" he has demonstrated a way of expression which can find a reality for man not limited by the material but which can exist and be heard in the midst of man's functioning on all levels.

The Precursors

Manuel González Prada

Manuel Gutiérrez Nájera

José Martí

Julián del Casal

José Asunción Silva

The Precursors

MANUEL GONZÁLEZ PRADA (1848-1918), PERU

González Prada was born of a rich, distinguished, Spanish family, Catholic and conservative in ideas. There were striking contrasts in his character and between him and his home and his city. His travels brought him in contact with the Indians, and he desired to reform conditions. He fought in the war against Chile and when Peru was defeated, he shut himself up in his house for the three years of Chilean occupation and devoted himself to writing. He gathered together a group of intellectual youths who encouraged nationalism. He went to Paris in 1891 and then to Spain, returning to Peru in 1898. Although he was forbidden by the government to write or speak, he increased these activities; he wrote verse for recreation. After his sudden death, he was acclaimed and honored and his name and example became the standard of the new generation.

González Prada was very versatile, revealing various moods and attitudes. He wrote biting epigrams, humorous verse and satire, love lyrics, exposition of his social ideas, and ballads dealing with Indian legends; he used various meters as well as free verse. He criticized exaggerated sentimentality, preferring beautiful tranquillity and dignified grief; he also criticized the empty eloquence of contemporary poetry. He believed art should express the inner harmony between the rhythm of words and the silent rhythm of ideas. He said renovation of poetry should include form, which had become poor and monotonous. He used free verse with varying rhythms and accents.

His *Peruvian Ballads* initiated the real indigenous poetry, beginning with the mythical origin of Peru and ending with its liberation by Bolívar's army. He denounced the exploitation of the Indians and peons, thus introducing social problems.

He wrote ballads and songs in the Germanic style in the 1870's; he introduced meters from the French, English, and Italian. He opened the way for different foreign influences to affect Peruvian literature.

"Wealth and Glory" and "Thine Eyes like Irises" are triolets; both have the same rhyme scheme, with the first verse being repeated two more times and the second verse once. The first expresses a disillusioned philosophy of life, probably stemming from the poet's own experiences. In the second the contrast between eyes and lips is not only physical but also sentimental.

"An Episode" has contrasts of color that also appear in "Thine Eyes Like Irises." This poem also illustrates the use of free verse with varying rhythms and accents; the ten verses range from nine to seventeen syllables. The death of the dove is just an "episode" compared to the processes of nature.

MANUEL GUTIÉRREZ NÁJERA (1859-1895), MEXICO

Gutiérrez Nájera was born in Mexico City of a middle class family. He attended a French school and was well trained in Latin. Throughout his adult life he was a journalist and also wrote stories and lyric prose and contributed to several literary periodicals. He founded the *Revista azul,* the first Modernist journal; he said he called it "blue" because blue is not merely a color, but also a mystery. Besides preferring the same color Gutiérrez Nájera and Rubén Darío were alike in their aristocratic nature, homely appearance, journalistic work, and seeking escape in drink. Gutiérrez Nájera used several pseudonyms, of which his favorite was "Duke Job," suggesting the aristocrat and the sufferer. He expected to die young, as he did. His French readings and the new liberalism, and the skeptic ideas of his time were in conflict with his orthodox Catholic training. He never attained calmness and a philosophical attitude. Many of his poems deal with his religious doubts and the enigma of life and death.

In his earliest verse he imitated Bécquer and Campoamor, but when he became acquainted with French literature, he attempted to "express French thoughts in Spanish verse," according to Justo Sierra. Although there are evidences of various French schools as well as of Romanticism in his work, he united them, making them his own and giving them a melancholy although elegant aspect and tone. Thus his work represents a transition between Romanticism and Modernism. In "To the Corregidor's Wife" he succeeded in imitating sounds by the vowels and consonants he used.

Although some critics doubt the sincerity of "When I Die," if one takes into consideration the conflict in the poet's own soul and his awareness of the fleeting aspect of life, his desire to die young does not seem unreasonable. He invests the idea of death with grace and beauty rather than the horror some poets present.

"Whiteness" is evidently influenced by Gautier's "Symphony in White Major," in which the poet enumerates white objects appearing in nature. The regular accent falling on every third syllable, starting with the second syllable of the line, is unusual in Spanish versification.

JOSÉ MARTÍ (1853-1895), CUBA

Martí, who was an educator, patriot, orator, journalist, revolutionary worker, and national hero as well as a writer, was born in Havana. He received his law degree in Spain where he had been banished in 1870 because of his seditious propaganda. He returned to America in 1875 and resided in Mexico, Guatemala, and Venezuela, collaborating on newspapers and reviews, and teaching. After being exiled again, he established his residence in New York in 1881 where he was employed by the *New York Sun.* He devoted the remainder of his life to the Cuban revolutionary party working for the independence of Cuba and Puerto Rico. When the revolution finally began, he perished in battle.

Martí himself pointed out two steps in the development of his poetry. The poems in *Free Verses,* written mostly in 1882, full of dazzling metaphors, were influenced by Campoamor and Bécquer. Those in *Simple Verses* (1891) were characterized by simplicity but with depths of thought. His poetry reveals his own personality and unquiet spirit along with his great energy, deep emotions, and high ideals. In the introduction to *Simple Verses* he says his verse comes from his heart; these poems were written in the mountains where he had been sent for his health. He skillfully employs the popular ballad meter but instead of assonance, he uses consonantal rhyme, which gives structural unity to each stanza. Children use that meter in the choruses of their games. One needs to understand Martí's own life in order to comprehend the symbolic truth of his poetry. Martí's contribution to Modernism was the simple form suggesting primitive art.

Number I of *Simple Verses* depicts Martí's emotions on many occasions and reveals a sensitive loving nature. He is more interested in the compassion the bailiff expresses than in the death penalty itself. In Number XXV Martí is all grief and melancholy without a fatherland, but he is also without a master; free, in a foreign land, he asks for flowers on his tomb, and by the use of the dash, he emphasizes what he most longs for—the flag. These are like the flowers and flag on the patriot's tomb in Mexico that he once described. Martí learned the use of the dash from the poet Mendive; it was mocked at in Mexico, according to Manuel Isidro Méndez. This critic suggests that the two stanzas could be separated into two poems, but by subtly uniting "I think" and "I wish," and by placing melancholy beside rejoicing and color, the poet attains a fine concordance. The symbolist leaves the thought a little vague so the reader can take pleasure in loving collaboration.

JULIÁN DEL CASAL (1863-1893), CUBA

Julián del Casal was born and died in Havana. His short life was very unhappy, due to grief over the death of his parents, comparative poverty, and his natural melancholy; he felt out of sympathy with the people around him and lived in his world of imagination. When he was introduced to the modern French writers, he "devoured" them and assimilated Parnassianism, Decadentism, and Symbolism. He became interested in the Orient and filled his small room with as many Japanese objects as possible. When he sold his small inheritance to finance a trip to Spain, he found that country in general not ready to appreciate his work and returned to Cuba, bitterly disillusioned. The one bright spot in his life was the visit of Darío to Havana in 1892, which profoundly impressed Casal. He became ill of tuberculosis in 1892 and died in 1893.

His first works had a decidedly romantic cast. As he became more objective and influenced by the French Parnassian school, he wrote with formal correctness, as in his sonnets describing the paintings of Gustave Moreau with rich colorful detail, and also persons and harbor scenes. His *Rhymes* (1893) reveal the desolation of Baudelaire, whom he read with some repulsion, but who left marks of his influence; Casal liked macabre detail, although in less degree than Baudelaire. He felt great ennui but also a horror of death. He displayed Modernist exoticism in his longing to see other climes. His cultivation of the beauty of form was also an important contribution to Modernism.

Casal experimented with versification; he used the monorhymed tercet and the verse of nine syllables. He often extended an item from one line to another, instead of ending each line with a complete division of thought. At times he repeated the beginning verse at the end of the stanza, making a sort of echo.

"Nihilism" expresses Casal's attitude toward life—one of utter boredom. It may have been inspired by Baudelaire. Evidently his conscience reproaches him for his indifference toward life, but he is unable, or unwilling, to attempt to overcome it.

"Pages from Life" is based on the farewell conversation he had with Rubén Darío as the latter is about to sail from Cuba. Darío addresses Casal in the first five stanzas, contrasting his philosophy of life with Casal's. The last two stanzas are Casal's own thoughts.

JOSÉ ASUNCIÓN SILVA (1865-1896), COLOMBIA

As a youth Silva was noted for his proud superiority and seriousness. He assisted his father in his luxurious shop of silks, perfumes, and porcelain and art objects. After two years of travel in Europe he returned with objects for the store and with a feeling of tedium. He organized a tertulia of intellectual youths, who read the brilliant European authors. Silva's father lost his fortune; when he died in 1889, José became the head of the family and attempted many rash projects to obtain money. He was handsome and dressed elegantly. He was interested in everything—arts, love, war, politics, etc. Although Silva pretended to enjoy life, Miguel de Unamuno summed up his life as "suffering, dreaming, singing." As poverty prevented the satisfaction of his many desires, he satisfied them only through dreams and rejected reality. In the conservative atmosphere of Bogotá he felt misunderstood and unappreciated. He suffered various misfortunes. Many of his writings were lost in a shipwreck. After his beautiful young sister, whom he loved very much, died, Silva became still more melancholy and finally shot himself in the heart.

Silva frequently finds his inspiration in dreams and memories of childhood, as he found disillusionment in human relationships. Various poems express this disillusionment. "Philosophies" describes the futility of the various fields of human endeavor—carnal pleasures, drink, work, art, religion, philosophies. "A Poem" suggests Silva's own technique. He dreams of composing a wonderful work, using the tragic, fantastic, subtle story of an idolized dead woman. He calls on all the rhythms and describes them.

He uses golden phrases and suggests strange music. In the vague light of the far away depths masked figures pass. Vague suggestions of mystic sentiment and human temptations pass across the background. The poet gives his verse the odor of heliotrope and the color of an amethyst.

Silva was typical of the Modernists in his longing to taste all experiences and in his feeling that he was misunderstood by his fellowmen. His verse was musical, and his metrical experiments did much to liberate Spanish-American poetry.

When "Nocturne" was published in a review in 1894, it aroused great interest with its free meter and repetitions. Many admired and imitated it and others ridiculed it mercilessly; the intellectual young women of Colombia laughed at it. Sanín Cano, Silva's friend, explained the motivation of the poem. When Silva's father died, the family went to an old estate in the country during the period of mourning. His sister Elvira was accustomed to walk with him at night along a path above which a steep hill arose; below and far away the plain of dry wheat extended, suggestive of incomparable melancholy. The full moon passing over the hills projected the shadows of the passersby as specters over the plain. The brother and sister often entertained themselves looking at the deformed and evanescent shadows. After the sister's death the family again went to the estate, and naturally the memory of their nocturnal walks obsessed Silva and resulted in the beautiful poem. The Spanish verse has feet of four syllables for the most part, with accent on the third syllable. Nouns of very rich emotional content are employed and the adjectives give even greater force. The ideas and emotions fade away in the shadow, sustained only by the rhythm. The typographical arrangement of the lines suggests the effect of shadow.

"Firewood of St. John" is based on children's rhymes; the changing meter is suited to the change in thought; the rhythm suggests the rocking motion of a child on the grandmother's knees. The philosopher's inquietude is revealed, even in a poem presumably representing a happy mood at the beginning.

Carlos E. Restrepo says that Silva reciting "The Response of the Earth," emphasized with a scornful smile and mordant irony the last two lines and affirmed he had written it because a poet friend had nonsensical notions about pantheism and talked to all the elements and the stars.

"Art" reveals the poet's concern with artistic principles.

"Stars" indicates his concern with the enigmas of life and nature.

MANUEL GONZALEZ PRADA

TRIOLET

Los bienes y las glorias de la vida
o nunca vienen o nos llegan tarde.
Lucen de cerca, pasan de corrida,
los bienes y las glorias de la vida.
¡Triste del hombre que en la edad florida
coger las flores del vivir aguarde!
Los bienes y las glorias de la vida
o nunca vienen o nos llegan tarde.

TRIOLET

Tus ojos de lirio dijeron que sí,
tus labios de rosa dijeron que no.
Al verme a tu lado, muriendo por ti,
tus ojos de lirio dijeron que sí.
Auroras de gozo rayaron en mí;
mas pronto la noche de luto volvió:
tus ojos de lirio dijeron que sí,
tus labios de rosa dijeron que no.

EPISODIO

(Polirritmo sin rima)

Feroces picotazos, estridentes aleteos,
con salvajes graznidos de victoria y muerte.

Revolotean blancas plumas
y el verde campo alfombran con tapiz de armiño;
en un azul de amor, de paz y gloria,
bullen alas negras y picos rojos.

Sucumbe la paloma, triunfa el ave de rapiña;
mas, luminoso, imperturbable, se destaca el firmamento,
y sigue en las entrañas de la eterna Madre
la gestación perenne de la vida.

MANUEL GONZALEZ PRADA

WEALTH AND GLORY

The wealth and glory that life can bestow
Will either never come or reach us late;
They come and shine quite near but quickly go,
The wealth and glory that life can bestow.
Alas for him who when the flowers grow
Neglects to pick them, thinking more await!
The wealth and glory that life can bestow
Will either never come or reach us late.

THINE EYES LIKE IRISES

Thine eyes like irises said "yes" to me;
Thy lips like crimson roses told me "no";
Seeing me near, dying because of thee,
Thine eyes like irises said "yes" to me.
The dawn of joy began to shine on me;
Then night's black mourning covered all below.
Thine eyes like irises said "yes" to me;
Thy lips like crimson roses told me "no."

AN EPISODE

(Polyrhythmic without rhyme)

Ferocious, vicious snaps of beaks and strident flaps of wings,
With savage cawing sounds of victory and death.

White feathers flutter to the earth
And carpet the green fields with tapestry of ermine;
Upon a field of glory, peace, and love,
Black wings and crimson beaks move in confusion.

The dove succumbing, perishes; the bird of prey is victor;
The firmament, however, stands out luminous and unperturbed,
And life's perennial gestation still continues
Within the depths of the eternal Mother.

MANUEL GUTIERREZ NAJERA

PARA ENTONCES

Quiero morir cuando decline el día,
en alta mar y con la cara al cielo;
donde parezca un sueño la agonía,
y el alma, un ave que remonta el vuelo.

No escuchar en los últimos instantes,
ya con el cielo y con la mar a solas,
más voces ni plegarias sollozantes
que el majestuoso tumbo de las olas.

Morir cuando la luz triste retira
sus áureas redes de la onda verde,
y ser como ese sol que lento expira:
algo muy luminoso que se pierde.

Morir, y joven: antes que destruya
el tiempo aleve la gentil corona;
cuando la vida dice aún: "soy tuya,"
¡aunque sepamos bien que nos traiciona!

DE BLANCO

¿Qué cosa más blanca que cándido lirio?
¿Qué cosa más pura que místico cirio?
¿Qué cosa más casta que tierno azahar?
¿Qué cosa más virgen que leve neblina?
¿Qué cosa más santa que el ara divina de gótico altar?

De blancas palomas el aire se puebla;
con túnica blanca, tejida de niebla,
se envuelve a lo lejos feudal torreón;
erguida en el huerto la trémula acacia
al soplo del viento sacude con gracia su níveo pompón.

MANUEL GUTIERREZ NAJERA

WHEN I DIE

I wish to die as some fair day is dying,
Upon the sea, my face turned toward the sky,
Where death's dread agony may seem a dream,
My soul, a bird that spreads its wings to fly.

To hear in those last moments that I live,
Accompanied by sky and sea alone,
No prayers nor voices broken by deep sobs,
But only rolling waves' majestic tone.

To die when fading light takes from the waves
Its golden nets and leaves a greenish hue;
To be just like the sun when slowly dying,
A radiance soon vanishing from view.

To die still young, before perfidious time
Destroys the blessed brightness of my days,
While life is still asserting, "I am yours,"
Although we know quite well that she betrays.

WHITENESS

What is whiter than lilies' immaculate white?
What is purer than tapers with mystical light?
What more virgin than mist as it drifts soft and fine?
What more chaste than the blossoms that orange-trees wear?
What more holy than stones on the altars that bear
The white Host, food divine?

Flocks of doves fill the atmosphere with their soft whiteness,
And a tunic of white that is made from mist's lightness
In the distance envelops the large feudal tower.
In the garden acacia trees' branches are quaking;
At the breath of a breeze thay are gracefully shaking
Every snowy white flower.

¿No ves en el monte la nieve que albea?
La torre muy blanca domina la aldea,
las tiernas ovejas triscando se van,
de cisnes intactos el lago se llena,
columpia su copa la enhiesta azucena,
y su ánfora inmensa levanta el volcán.

Entremos al templo: la hostia fulgura;
de nieve parecen las canas del cura,
vestido con alba de lino sutil;
cien niñas hermosas ocupan las bancas,
y todas vestidas con túnicas blancas
en ramos ofrecen las flores de abril.

Subamos al coro: la virgen propicia
escucha los rezos de casta novicia,
y el cristo de mármol expira en la cruz;
sin mancha se yerguen las velas de cera;
de encaje es la tenue cortina ligera
que ya transparenta del alba la luz.

Bajemos al campo: tumulto de plumas
parece el arroyo de blancas espumas
que quieren, cantando, correr y saltar;
la airosa mantilla de fresca neblina
terció la montaña; la vela latina
de barca ligera se pierde en el mar.

Ya salta del lecho la joven hermosa,
y el agua refresca sus hombros de diosa,
sus brazos ebúrneos, su cuello gentil;
cantando y risueña se ciñe la enagua,
y trémulas brillan las gotas de agua
en su árabe peine de blanco marfil.

¡Oh mármol! ¡Oh nieves! ¡Oh inmensa blancura
que esparces doquiera tu casta hermosura!
¡Oh tímida virgen! ¡Oh casta vestal!
Tú estás en la estatua de eterna belleza;
de tu hábito blando nació la pureza,
¡al ángel das alas, sudario al mortal!

Do you see on the mountain the whitening of snow?
The white tower commands the whole village below;
Flocks of gentle white sheep now go gamboling by;
Swans display on the lake their immaculate down;
The tall lily is swinging her flowery crown;
The volcano is holding its amphora high.

Let us enter the temple; thc Host has a glow;
The white hair of the priest has the semblance of snow,
And his alb is of linen of exquisite weave;
On the benches a hundred fair girls dressed in white
Are holding bouquets of spring flowers so bright,
The pure offerings that they will joyously leave.

Let us go to the choir; there the Virgin so fair
Hears propitiatory the novice's prayer,
And the white marble Christ on the crucifix dies;
All the tapers of wax stand so spotless and straight;
The light curtain of lace is so gauzy in weight
That the brightness shines through from the dawn's rosy skies.

Let us go to the country; white plume heaped on plume
In confusion is only the brook's snowy spume
That while singing is striving to run and to leap;
The cool mist has created a delicate veil
For the mountain's mantilla; the white lateen sail
That impels the swift ship disappears on the deep.

The fair maiden now leaps from her bed and applies
Cooling water to shoulders a goddess might prize,
Her white arms, and her neck, which is graceful and fair;
Then she dons her white petticoat, laughing and singing;
Trembling droplets of water are shining, still clinging
To the ivory Arabic comb in her hair.

O soft snow! O pure marble! O infinite whiteness,
You bestow everywhere your own lovely chaste brightness!
O shy nun! O pure vestal to chastity vowed!
You are part of the beauty that statues possess;
And sweet purity's home is your lovely soft dress.
You give wings to the angels and mankind, a shroud!

Tú cubres al niño que llega a la vida,
coronas las sienes de fiel prometida,
al paje revistes de rico tisú.
¡Qué blancos son, reinas, los mantos de armiño!
¡Qué blanca es, ¡oh madres! la cuna del niño!
¡Qué blanca, mi amada, qué blanca eres tú!

En sueños ufanos de amores contemplo
alzarse muy blancas las torres de un templo
y oculto entre lirios abrirse un hogar;
y el velo de novia prenderse a tu frente,
cual nube de gasa que cae lentamente,
y viene a tus hombros su encaje a posar.

You envelop the babe in his first hour of life;
And you crown the white brow of the fair promised wife;
You dress pages in cloth of a silvery hue.
Oh how white is the ermine that queens proudly wear!
Oh how white are the cradles that mothers prepare!
Oh how white, my beloved, how white you are too!

I behold in my dreams of the joys of true love
A white temple with very white towers above,
And concealed midst white lilies, a home offers brightness;
The soft veil of a bride is pinned over your brow;
Like a cloud of light gauze it descends slowly now
And its lace comes to rest on your shoulders' soft whiteness.

JOSE MARTI

VERSOS SENCILLOS

I

Yo soy un hombre sincero
de donde crece la palma;
y antes de morirme, quiero
echar mis versos del alma.

Yo vengo de todas partes,
y hacia todas partes voy:
arte soy entre las artes;
en los montes, monte soy.

Yo sé los nombres extraños
de las yerbas y las flores,
y de mortales engaños,
y de sublimes dolores.

Yo he visto en la noche oscura
llover sobre mi cabeza
los rayos de lumbre pura
de la divina belleza.

Alas nacer vi en los hombros
de las mujeres hermosas,
y salir de los escombros,
volando, las mariposas.

He visto vivir a un hombre
con el puñal al costado,
sin decir jamás el nombre
de aquella que lo ha matado.

Rápida, como un reflejo,
dos veces vi el alma, dos:
cuando murió el pobre viejo,
cuando ella me dijo adiós.

JOSE MARTI

SIMPLE VERSES

I

I am a man who is sincere,
From where palms grow abundantly;
And I desire before I die
To utter my soul's poetry.

I come from all localities
And go to all of them anew;
Among the arts I am an art;
Midst mountains am a mountain too.

I know the strange and foreign names
Of every flower, herb, and grass,
And of illusions and great griefs
Through which each mortal man must pass.

I have observed on some dark nights
There seemed to rain upon my head
Some vivid rays of purest light,
That superhuman beauty shed.

I saw how growing on the shoulders
Of lovely women, wings arise,
And coming out of some debris
To wing their flight, were butterflies.

One time I saw a man still living
Who had a dagger in his side,
But never would divulge the name
Of her who was the homicide.

I saw the soul two times, yes two,
As rapid as reflections fly:
The time the poor old man expired,
And when she said to me, "good-bye."

Temblé una vez—en la reja,
a la entrada de la viña —,
cuando la bárbara abeja
picó en la frente a mi niña.

Gocé una vez, de tal suerte
que gocé cual nunca: cuando
la sentencia de mi muerte
leyó el alcaide llorando.

Oigo un suspiro a través
de las tierras y la mar,
y no es un suspiro: es
que mi hijo va a despertar.

Si dicen que del joyero
tome la joya mejor,
tomo a un amigo sincero
y pongo a un lado el amor.

Yo he visto al águila herida
volar al azul sereno,
y morir en su guarida
la víbora del veneno.

Yo sé bien que cuando el mundo
cede, lívido, al descanso,
sobre el silencio profundo
murmura el arroyo manso.

Yo he puesto la mano osada,
de horror y júbilo yerta,
sobre la estrella apagada
que cayó frente a mi puerta.

Oculto en mi pecho bravo
la pena que me lo hiere:
el hijo de un pueblo esclavo
vive por él, calla y muere.

One time I trembled,—at the grating
That makes the vineyard's entrance way;
My little daughter's brow was stung
By some barbaric bee that day.

I once rejoiced as I had never
Rejoiced before in all my years:
When my death penalty was read,
The bailiff reading it shed tears.

I now can hear a sigh that comes
Across the lands, across the deep,
And it is not a sigh: it means
My son begins to rouse from sleep.

If they tell me to take the jewel
That is the jeweller's great pride,
I then shall take a friend that's true,
And place my love off to one side.

I have observed the wounded eagle
That soared to tranquil heights again,
And have observed the deadly viper
Expire from poison in his den.

I know well when the world, turned livid,
Submits to restful interlude,
The gentle little brook still murmurs
Above the deepest quietude.

I have laid down my daring hand,
Inert from happiness and dread,
Upon the meteor that fell
Before my door from overhead.

I hide whatever pains that wound me,
So in my fearless heart they lie;
The son of people in enslavement
Must live for them, be silent, die.

Todo es hermoso y constante,
todo es música y razón,
y todo, como el diamante,
antes que luz es carbón.

Yo sé que el necio se entierra
con gran lujo y con gran llanto,
y que no hay fruta en la tierra
como la del camposanto.

Callo, y entiendo, y me quito
la pompa del rimador;
cuelgo de un árbol marchito
mi muceta de doctor.

XXV

Yo pienso, cuando me alegro
como un escolar sencillo,
en el canario amarillo —
¡que tiene el ojo tan negro!

Yo quiero, cuando me muera,
sin patria, pero sin amo,
tener en mi losa un ramo
de flores—¡y una bandera!

All things are beautiful and constant,
All things are music and are right,
And all of them, like diamonds,
Are carbon, ere they turn to light.

I know that when the fool is buried,
There is great pomp and weeping there;
I know there is no fruit on earth
Like that the cemeteries bear.

I, silent, think and lay aside
The pomp of making poetry;
I hang on this dry tree my hood
That means the doctoral degree.

XXV

I think, when I am of good cheer
As simple schoolboys are when merry,
About the yellow-hued canary,
And oh how black its eyes appear!

I wish that when I come to die,
Without a fatherland, but free,
That on my gravestone there may be
Some flowers,—and a flag to fly!

JULIAN DEL CASAL

NIHILISMO

Voz inefable que a mi estancia llega
en medio de las sombras de la noche,
por arrastrarme hacia la vida, brega
con las dulces cadencias del reproche.

¿A qué llamarme al campo del combate
con la promesa de terrenos bienes,
si ya mi corazón por nada late
ni oigo la idea martillar mis sienes?

Nadie extrañe mis ásperas querellas:
mi vida, atormentada de rigores,
es un cielo que nunca tuvo estrellas,
es un árbol que nunca tuvo flores.

De todo lo que he amado en este mundo
guardo, como perenne recompensa,
dentro del corazón, tedio profundo;
dentro del pensamiento, sombra densa.

Nada del porvenir a mi alma asombra
y nada del presente juzgo bueno;
si miro al horizonte, todo es sombra,
si me inclino a la tierra, todo es cieno.

Ansias de aniquilarme sólo siento,
o de vivir en mi eternal pobreza,
con mi fiel compañero, el descontento,
y mi pálida novia, la tristeza.

JULIAN DEL CASAL

NIHILISM

Ineffable voice that midst the shades of night
Arriving in the place where I abide,
Dost strive to draw me into life itself,
As thy sweet cadences so gently chide.

Why dost thou call me to the field of strife
With promises of earthly good to gain,
If now my heart will palpitate for naught,
And thought no longer beats within my brain?

May my morose complaints astonish none;
My life tormented by some rigid power,
Is as a sky that never had a star,
Is as a tree that never had a flower.

Of all that I have loved within this world
I keep as my perennial recompense,
Within my heart the greatest tedium,
Within my thoughts, a darkness most intense.

Naught in the future can astound my soul,
And I judge nothing present good and right;
On looking at the sky, I see but shadows,
If I look earthward, mire then meets my sight.

I long but to annihilate myself,
Or else in poverty as now abide,
With discontent, my ever true companion,
And my pale sweetheart, sadness, at my side.

PAGINAS DE VIDA

—Yo soy como esas plantas que ignota mano
siembra un día en el surco por donde marcha,
ya para que la anime luz de verano,
ya para que la hiele frío de escarcha.

. . . .

Mas como nada espero lograr del hombre,
y en la bondad divina mi ser confía,
aunque llevo en el alma penas sin nombre,
no siento la nostalgia de la alegría.

¡Ígnea columna sigue mi paso cierto!
¡Salvadora creencia mi ánimo salva!
¡Yo sé que tras las olas me aguarda el puerto!
¡Yo sé que tras la noche surgirá el alba!

Tú en cambio, que doliente mi voz escuchas,
sólo el hastío llevas dentro del alma:
juzgándote vencido por nada luchas
y de ti se desprende siniestra calma.

. . . .

Si hubiéramos más tiempo juntos vivido,
no nos fuera la ausencia tan dolorosa.
¡Tú cultivas tus males, yo el mío olvido!
¡Tú lo ves todo en negro, yo todo en rosa!

. . . .

Genio errante, vagando de clima en clima,
sigue el rastro fulgente de un espejismo,
con el ansia de alzarse siempre a la cima,
mas también con el vértigo que da el abismo.

. . . .

Doblegado en la tierra luego de hinojos,
miro cuanto a mi lado gozoso existe
y pregunto, con lágrimas en los ojos,
¿por qué has hecho ¡oh Dios mío! mi alma tan triste?

PAGES FROM LIFE

"I am just like those plants whose seeds some stranger sows
Within the furrow as he passes by one day;
Perchance the light of summer may provide them life;
Perchance the cold of frost may freeze their life away.

"But as I have no hopes for anything from man,
And base my trust on God's benevolence alone,
Though I am bearing nameless sorrows in my soul,
I do not long for joys that I have ever known.

"I follow with sure step a pillar of bright fire!
My soul will be redeemed through faith's great wondrous might!
I know beyond the waves a port awaits me there!
I know beyond the darkness comes the dawn's fair light!

"You, on the other hand, that grieving hear my voice,
Your soul bears naught but tedium of all around;
You, judging your own self defeated, fight no more;
Your very calmness is unwholesome and unsound.

"If we had lived together for a longer time,
Our separation would not be so sad to view,
You cultivate your ills; and I forget my woes!
You see all as if black; I, all with rosy hue."

You, roaming genius, wandering from clime to clime,
Still cherish your illusions with their promised bliss,
With longing always to ascend to greatest heights,
But seized with vertigo on seeing the abyss.

Now as I am on bended knees upon the earth,
I look at everything around me that is glad,
And ask the question as the tears come to my eyes,
"O God, why is it Thou has made my soul so sad?"

JOSE ASUNCION SILVA

NOCTURNO (III)

Una noche,
una noche toda llena de murmullos, de perfumes y de músicas de alas;
una noche
en que ardían en la sombra nupcial y húmeda las luciérnagas fantásticas,
a mi lado lentamente, contra mí ceñida toda, muda y pálida,
como si un presentimiento de amarguras infinitas
hasta el más secreto fondo de las fibras te agitara,
por la senda florecida que atraviesa la llanura
caminabas;
y la luna llena
por los cielos azulosos, infinitos y profundos esparcía su luz blanca;
y tu sombra
fina y lánguida,
y mi sombra,
por los rayos de la luna proyectadas,
sobre las arenas tristes
de la senda se juntaban;
y eran una,
y eran una,
y eran una sola sombra larga,
y eran una sola sombra larga,
y eran una sola sombra larga. . .

Esta noche
solo; el alma
llena de las infinitas amarguras y agonías de tu muerte,
separado de ti misma por el tiempo, por la tumba y la distancia,

JOSE ASUNCION SILVA

NOCTURNE

On a night,
On a night full of murmuring sounds, sweet aromas, and music of wings;
On a night
When fantastical fireflies were shedding their glow in the damp nuptial shadow,
At my side with slow step, pressing closely against me in silence and pallid,
Just as if a presentiment, warning of infinite bitterness,
Were disturbing you down to the most secret depths of your being,
On the pathway bedecked with bright blossoms, that crosses the plain,
You were walking;
And the moon at its full
Was then spreading its colorless light through the infinite fathomless heavens;
And your shadow,
Fine and languid,
And my shadow,
There projected by rays of the moon,
On the sorrowful sands
Of the path were united,
And were one,
And were one,
And were one single long drawn out shadow,
And were one single long drawn out shadow,
And were one single long drawn out shadow. . .

Now tonight,
Solitary,
With my soul overflowing with sorrow and bitterness caused by your death,
Separated from you by the passage of time, by the tomb, by the distance,

por el infinito negro
donde nuestra voz no alcanza,
mudo y solo
por la senda caminaba...
y se oían los ladridos de los perros a la luna,
a la luna pálida,
y el chirrido
de las ranas...
Sentí frío. Era el frío que tenían en tu alcoba
tus mejillas y tus sienes y tus manos adoradas,
entre las blancuras níveas
de las mortuorias sábanas.
Era el frío del sepulcro, era el hielo de la muerte,
era el frío de la nada.
Y mi sombra,
por los rayos de la luna proyectada,
iba sola,
iba sola,
iba sola por la estepa solitaria;
y tu sombra esbelta y ágil,
fina y lánguida,
como en esa noche tibia de la muerta primavera,
como en esa noche llena de murmullos, de perfumes y de músicas de alas,
se acercó y marchó con ella,
se acercó y marchó con ella,
se acercó y marchó con ella... ¡Oh las sombras enlazadas!
¡Oh las sombras de los cuerpos que se juntan con las sombras de las almas!
¡Oh las sombras que se buscan en las noches de tristezas y de lágrimas!

By the infinite blackness
Where our voice does not reach;
Mute and lonely.
I walked there on the path. . .
And the noise could be heard of the barking of dogs at the moon,
At the moon in its pallor,
And the croaking
Of the frogs. . .
I felt cold. And that cold was the same that was there in your bedroom
On your cheeks, on your temples, and also your hands so adored,
Midst the whiteness of snow
Of the funeral sheets.
That was cold of the sepulcher, glacial coldness of death,
That was coldness of nothingness.
And my shadow,
There projected by rays of the moon,
Went alone,
Went alone,
Went alone on the plain that was barren and lonely;
And your tall agile shadow,
Fine and languid,
As it was on that mild cloudless night of the springtime now dead,
On that night full of murmuring sounds, sweet aromas, and music of wings,
Drawing near, walked beside it,
Drawing near, walked beside it,
Drawing near, walked beside it. . .Oh the shadows that join to form one!
Oh the shadows of bodies that join with the shadows of souls!
Oh the shadows that seek one another on sad tearful nights!

LOS MADEROS DE SAN JUAN

. . .Y aserrín
aserrán,
los maderos
de San Juan
piden queso,
piden pan;
los de Roque,
Alfandoque;
los de Rique,
Alfeñique;
los de Trique,
Triquitrán.
¡Triqui, triqui, triqui, tran!
¡Triqui, triqui, triqui, tran. . .

Y en las rodillas duras y firmes de la abuela
con movimiento rítmico se balancea el niño,
y entrambos agitados y trémulos están. . .
La abuela se sonríe con maternal cariño,
mas cruza por su espíritu como un temor extraño
por lo que en el futuro, de angustia y desengaño,
los días ignorados del nieto guardarán. . .

Los maderos
de San Juan
piden queso,
piden pan;
¡Triqui, triqui, triqui, tran!

¡Esas arrugas hondas recuerdan una historia
de largos sufrimientos y silenciosa angustia!,
y sus cabellos blancos como la nieve están;
. . .de un gran dolor el sello marcó la frente mustia,
y son sus ojos turbios espejos que empañaron
los años, y que a tiempo las formas reflejaron
de seres y de cosas que nunca volverán. . .

THE FIREWOOD OF ST. JOHN

. . .And aserrín
Aserrán;
Firewood gathered
For St. John
Asks for cheese now,
Bread anon;
That of Roque,
Alfandoque;
That of Rique,
Alfeñique;
That of Trique,
Triquitrán;
Triqui, triqui, triqui, tran!
Triqui, triqui, triqui, tran! . . .

Held by the grandmother on her hard steady knees
The child is swinging back and forth with rhythmic motion,
And both of them are tremulous and agitated.
The grandmother's sweet smile shows motherly devotion,
But something passes through her mind that seems strange fear
For future pains and disillusions to appear,
That her small grandson must endure, whenever fated. . .

Firewood gathered
For St. John
Asks for cheese now,
Bread anon;
Triqui, triqui, triqui, tran!

Those deepened wrinkles bring to mind a history
Of suffering prolonged and anguish mutely borne!
Her hair looks like the snow, it has become so hoar;
Upon her withered brow great sorrow's stamp is worn;
Her eyes are darkened mirrors blurred by years that passed,
Within whose depths reflections formerly were cast
Of beings and of things that will return no more. . .

. . .Los de Roque,
Alfandoque. . .
¡Triqui, triqui, triqui, tran!

Mañana, cuando duerma la abuela, yerta y muda,
lejos del mundo vivo, bajo la oscura tierra,
donde otros, en la sombra, desde hace tiempo están,
del nieto a la memoria, con grave voz que encierra
todo el poema triste de la remota infancia,
pasando por las sombras del tiempo y la distancia,
de aquella voz querida las notas volverán. . .

. . .Los de Rique,
Alfeñique. . .
¡Triqui, triqui, triqui, tran!. . .

En tanto, en las rodillas cansadas de la abuela
con movimiento rítmico se balancea el niño,
y entrambos agitados y trémulos están. . .
La abuela se sonríe con maternal cariño,
mas cruza por su espíritu como un temor extraño
por lo que en el futuro, de angustia y desengaño,
los días ignorados del nieto guardarán. . .

. . .Los maderos
de San Juan
piden queso,
piden pan;
los de Roque,
Alfandoque;
los de Rique,
Alfeñique;
los de Trique,
Triquitrán,
¡Triqui, triqui, triqui, tran!

. . .That of Roque,
Alfandoque. . .
Triqui, triqui, triqui, tran!

Tomorrow when the grandmother is mute and lifeless,
Below the earth, far from the world of life, reposing,
Where others have been in the dark since days of yore,
The grandson will recall a sober voice enclosing
The whole sad poem of remotest infancy,
As passing through great space and time's obscurity,
The tones of that beloved voice return once more. . .

. . .That of Rique,
Alfeñique. . .
Triqui, triqui, triqui, tran!

But now while seated on the grandmother's tired knees,
The child is swinging back and forth with rhythmic motion,
And both of them are tremulous and agitated.
The grandmother's sweet smile shows motherly devotion,
But something passes through her mind that seems strange fear,
For future pains and disillusions to appear,
That her small grandson must endure whenever fated. . .

. . .Firewood gathered
For St. John
Asks for cheese now,
Bread anon;
That of Roque,
Alfandoque,
That of Rique,
Alfeñique;
That of Trique,
Triquitrán,
Triqui, triqui, triqui, tran!

LA RESPUESTA DE LA TIERRA

Era un poeta lírico, grandioso y sibilino
que le hablaba a la tierra una tarde de invierno,
frente de una posada y al volver de un camino:
—Oh madre, oh tierra!—díjole,—en tu girar eterno
nuestra existencia efímera tal parece que ignoras.
Nosotros esperamos un cielo o un infierno,
sufrimos o gozamos en nuestras breves horas,
e indiferente y muda, tú, madre sin entraño
de acuerdo con los hombres no sufres y no lloras.
¿No sabes el secreto misterioso que entrañas?
¿Por qué las noches negras, las diáfanas auroras?
Las sombras vagarosas y tenues de unas cañas
que se reflejan lívidas en los estanques yertos,
¿no son como conciencias fantásticas y extrañas
que les copian sus vidas en espejos inciertos?
¿Qué somos? ¿A do vamos? ¿Por qué hasta aquí vivimos?
¿Conocen los secretos del más allá los muertos?
¿Por qué la vida inútil y triste recibimos?
¿Hay un oasis húmedo después de estos desiertos?
¿Por qué nacemos, madre, dime, por qué morimos?
¿Por qué? Mi angustia sacia y a mi ansiedad contesta.
Yo, sacerdote tuyo, arrodillado y trémulo,
en estas soledades aguardo la respuesta.

La tierra, como siempre, displicente y callada,
al gran poeta lírico no le contestó nada.

ARS

El verso es vaso santo; poned en él tan sólo
un pensamiento puro,
en cuyo fondo bullan hirvientes las imágenes
como burbujas de oro de un viejo vino obscuro.

THE RESPONSE OF THE EARTH

He was a lyric poet, sibylline, grandiloquent,
Who on returning from a journey made these observations
Before an inn one winter night with serious intent:
"O earth, O mother, during your continuous gyrations,
Regarding our ephemeral existence you seem blind.
A heaven or infernal regions are our expectations;
In our brief hours we suffer or some great delight we find;
And you, a heartless mother, mute, indifferent remain;
You do not weep or suffer, sympathizing with mankind.
Do you not know the secret mystery that you contain?
Why are the nights all black, and why is light to dawn assigned?
Is it not true those flickering, faint shadows of the cane
That are reflected lividly within the stagnant pond,
Resemble beings with strange minds of a fantastic vein,
To whose own lives reflections in dim mirrors correspond?
What are we? Why this life? Where do we go when it is past?
Do dead men know at last the secrets of the great beyond?
Why were we given useless life with sorrow overcast?
Can an oasis follow deserts where we now despond?
Why are we born, O mother? Say; why do we die at last?
Reply to my anxiety and soothe my anguish. Why?
  Now kneeling in this solitary place and trembling, I,
  Your dedicated priest, am here awaiting your reply."

The earth remained, as always, mute and peevishly distraught;
Her answer to the famous lyric poet then was naught.

ART

Verse is a sacred vase; deposit your thoughts there
That are most pure and fine,
Within whose depths ebullient imagery is stirring
Like golden bubbles rising in the dark old wine.

Allí verted las flores que la continua lucha
ajó del mundo frío,
recuerdos deliciosos de tiempos que no vuelven,
y nardos empapados en gotas de rocío.

Para que la existencia mísera se enbalsame
cual de una ciencia ignota,
quemándose en el fuego del alma enternecida
de aquel supremo bálsamo, ¡basta una sola gota!

...?...

Estrellas que entre lo sombrío
de lo ignorado y de lo inmenso,
asemejáis en el vacío
jirones pálidos de incienso;
nebulosas que ardéis tan lejos
en el infinito que aterra,
que sólo alcanzan los reflejos
de vuestra luz hasta la tierra;
astros que en abismos ignotos
derramáis resplandores vagos,
constelaciones que en remotos
tiempos adoraron los magos;
millones de mundos lejanos,
flores de fantástico broche,
islas claras en los océanos
sin fin ni fondo de la noche;
¡estrellas, luces pensativas!
¡Estrellas, pupilas inciertas!
¿Por qué os calláis si estáis vivas,
y por qué alumbráis si estáis muertas?

Pour there the flowers that the cold world's constant strife
Has crumpled hitherto,
Sweet memories of times that will return no more,
And also spikenard that is drenched in drops of dew.

So sad existence may receive perfume as though
From science still unknown,
When kindled in the fire within a tender soul,
One drop of that strong balsam will suffice alone.

STARS

O stars amidst the somberness
Of all the boundless and unknown,
You seem pale shreds of incense there,
Appearing in the void alone;
You nebulae so far away
In boundlessness that terrifies,
That only your reflected light
Can reach to where our planet lies;
O stars whose softly shining rays
Are in unknown abysses poured;
O constellations that the Magi
In distant temples once adored;
O millions of remotest worlds,
How strange a brooch your flowers adorn!
O shining islands of night's seas,
So fathomless and with no bourne!
O stars, soft meditative lights!
O eyes that flicker overhead!
Why are you silent if alive?
Why do you shine if you are dead?

The Modernists

Rubén Darío

Ricardo Jaimes Freyre

Amado Nervo

Leopoldo Lugones

José Santos Chocano

Julio Herrera y Reissig

Enrique González Martínez

The Modernists

RUBÉN DARÍO (1867-1916), NICARAGUA

Darío was of Spanish-Indian-Negro extraction. His poetic instinct seems to have guided him in assuming the rhythmical name of Rubén Darío, justified by the fact that an ancestor was called *Don Darío*, and Rubén's father used the name in business enterprises. He was reared by an aunt in a gloomy house; he said he knew pain from childhood; he liked to be alone, looking at the sky and the sea. He soon became known as the boy poet of Central America. He also began at an early age his series of love affairs and consequent disillusionments. His position in the National Library permitted him to read extensively in Spanish literature. He served as a journalist in various countries and in 1892 went to Spain, where he won the friendship of important authors and critics. Being appointed a consul from Colombia to Buenos Aires, he first visited New York, meeting Martí, and Paris, where he met Verlaine. *La Nación* of Buenos Aires sent him to various European countries; he was Nicaraguan consul in Paris and minister plenipotentiary in Madrid, besides other activities. He was acclaimed for his literary work wherever he went. Returning to America in ill health, he suffered an attack of pneumonia in New York and died in Nicaragua in 1916. His friend Vargas Vila said Darío was always a sad, radiant child, with genius' glance.

His first works were conservative and showed distaste for common people, whom he considered dull and evil. *Azure* (1888), a collection of poetry and stories in poetic prose, definitely Parnassian in technique, won the approval of the Spanish critic Juan Valera, who called him the most French author of Spanish works. Darío considered this collection a work of innovation because he abandoned the usual word order and conventional clichés and introduced novel uses of adjectives, based on his study of French Parnassian writers; he used fifteen-syllable and twelve-syllable verse and the free sonnet. He paid attention to the inner melody of the verse and said, as each word has a soul, there should be a melody of ideas accompanying the sound.

Lay Hymns (1896) established Modernism in Spanish America. José Enrique Rodó said Darío's poetry sounded like the song of a rite not understood; he saw intensely but only the delicate aspects of the material world, closing his eyes to the vulgar. He had an instinct for luxury, delighting in the use of silk, gold, and marble for comparisons. The lily would be his symbolic flower and the swan would be his symbolic bird engraved on his coat of arms; he would never be popular or care to be. In the preface, Darío says if there is any poetry in America it will be found in the old things—Indian legends, sensual and fine Incas, and great Montezuma in his gold chair; he adds, "The rest is yours, democratic Walt Whitman." Many inferior poets had been imitating his work and he was asked for a manifesto, which he refused, saying his literature was "mine in me" and no one should try to follow him slavishly. Among the technical innovations of this volume appear new strophic forms, metrical interruption of syntax, and free movement of the caesura, although many of his so-called innovations were merely renovations.

By the time *Songs of Life and Hope* (1905) appeared, Darío was ready to leave his ivory tower; he traces his own poetic development in the introductory poem. "The Optimist's Exhortation," written in classic hexameters, appeals to all of Spanish blood to throw off sloth and unite to win glory. "To Roosevelt" reveals fear of aggression by the United States. However, in a later poem, "Hail to the Eagle," he would like for the Latin race to learn constancy, vigor, and character from the Yankees; this poem appears in *The Errant Song* (1907), which reveals the poet as interested in universal feelings rather than personal emotions. Although Darío boasted of atheism, his primitive faith was always evident, and some of his later poems reveal true mysticism.

Darío frequently mentions the swan in his poetry. In "Heraldry" he describes its short eucharistic wing and its white neck shaped like the arm of a lyre. It is made of perfume, ermine, dawn, silk, and dreams. Rodó says that this is the first call to the swan; and the image of Leda, the swan of the South, arises. With the second call in "The Swan," the swan of the North arises. The swan's song is traditionally the symbol of twilight, but in Darío's poem it symbolizes the revelation of new light, and in its white plumage is the emblem of clarity of form. The swan is the least earthly and most aristocratic bird, associated with the delicate things of tradition. Rodó thinks Darío must have the blood of the swan in his blue veins. Darío tells in his *History of My Books* that he was initiated into the Wagnerian secrets in Buenos Aires in 1893 by a Belgian musician and writer, M. Charles de Gouffre. Wagner's *Lohengrin* became widely known in 1887 when performed in Paris. Argantir was a warrior owning a sword that was handed down from father to son in Icelandic tradition. Leconte de Lisle had written a poem about it. Since the swan represents absolute Beauty with no utilitarian ends, it became in Modernist poetry the symbol of the ideal and pure. Darío made the fourteen-syllable sonnet very popular.

"Sonatina" is appropriately named as it is very musical with its flowing rhythm and melodious words. Arturo Marasso Rocca suggests that the inspiration for the details came from the illustrated codices. In medieval manuscripts the month of May appears as a knight with his sword in his belt and his hawk on his hand, although his horse is not winged. The duenna, buffoon, distaff, and falcon are medieval motifs. The dragon comes from fairy tales and Scandinavian sagas. The geographical distribution of the flowers is capricious. The princess may be our soul, unquiet because of a vague desire for flight. Another interpretation is that she typifies the young maiden in love with love.

"Fatalism" reveals Darío's terror of the unknown that had obsessed him since childhood. In his *History of My Books* he admits that in this poem, against his deep-rooted religiosity and in spite of himself, there rises like a frightful shadow a phantom of desolation and doubt; he finds his Christian faith too weak.

RICARDO JAIMES FREYRE (1872-1933), BOLIVIA

Ricardo Jaimes Freyre's father was a writer, journalist, and teacher. Both father and son were good friends of Rubén Darío in Buenos Aires, and the three took interesting trips to a picturesque island. Ricardo and Darío were interested in French Symbolism, D'Annunzio, and Pre-Raphaelitism, as well as in old Spanish writers, as Darío tells in his autobiography. They founded the *Revista de América,* an organ of Modernism which had a short existence because of financial difficulties. Ricardo then published his *Pagan Fount,* which Darío calls one of the best and most brilliant examples of the efforts of the renovators, revealing a "powerful, delicate lyricism, wise in technique, and elevated in inspiration."

Jaimes Freyre was a professor of history and literature in the University of Tucumán, Argentina. In 1923 he was appointed Bolivian minister to the United States. Arturo Capdevila calls him "the marquis" because of his bearing, his words, and the impression he gave.

Pagan Fount (1899), his best work, is an innovation in exotic themes, as the poems of this collection deal with northern mythology, the gods and heroes of Valhalla, and the Wagnerian cycle. "Eternal Farewell" presents the advent of Christianity from the standpoint of the old Scandinavians who witness the downfall of their gods. In "Portico" the poet thinks it would be "beautiful" to live in the past heroic age as a monk, a churl, a minstrel, or a warrior; he idealizes the medieval times. His pictures are rather somber with gloomy forests, dark clouds, and night, but there are flashes of light at intervals. His innovations in meter exerted great influence on young Argentine poets. He initiated free verse in his poetry.

Jaimes Freyre presented his own theory of versification in his *Laws of Spanish Versification* (1912). He considered the fundamental unit of verse a block of from one to seven syllables with the fixed accent on the last syllable of each group. Blocks of different lengths may be used in the same poem if they all have either an odd or an even number of syllables. In regard to free verse, he believed each line represented one phase in the development of the complete thought or picture.

E. Solar Correa says that the rhythm of "The Sad Voices" does not correspond to external rules but is born from a certain state of soul and the theme itself, and the measure follows the variations of rhythm, forging a most unusual metrical combination. The music of the verse is not in the definite distribution of syllables but in the harmony of emotion with the words. There is a certain muffled music, a certain absence of color and sound that evoke marvelously the white infinitude of the steppe. He employs assonance, using grave vowels almost exclusively. Even the typographical form of very long verses contrasting with others very short produces a visual suggestion of the desolate Russian steppe, prolonged into the unending distance. Capdevila says the desolate region here presented is that of Potosí.

"Fleetingness" is pleasing with the music of the irregular combination of lines of seven and eleven syllables and its symbolism.

AMADO NERVO (1870-1919), MEXICO

Amado Nervo, the mystic poet, considered his name of value to his literary fortunes. He was destined for the church but for some reason gave up that vocation before taking his vows; Santiago Argüello says when Nervo left off his habit, it clung within him; he lived his asceticism as a poet and as a man. He traveled widely and followed various professions; he was a journalist, educator, diplomat, translator, and writer of short stories as well as of poetry. He settled in Mexico City in 1894 and wrote for the *Revista azul;* later he and Jesùs E. Valenzuela founded the *Revista moderna.* He went to Europe in 1901 and he traveled some with Darío. In 1905 he was appointed secretary of the Mexican Legation in Madrid and held that post for thirteen years. In 1918 he was sent as an envoy to Argentina and Uruguay and died in Montevideo in 1919.

Exodus and the Flowers along the Way (1902) shows Modernist influence. His mysticism is revealed in *Sister Water,* an early poem, in which the different forms of water running under the earth and those running over the earth describe their functions and all say, "Let us praise the Lord." His collections *Serenity* (1914) and *Elevation* (1916) reveal his deviation from the Modernist striving for beautiful ideas and form; he expresses commonplaces in a simple, sincere manner, sometimes too simple and unpoetic, but at other times very effective and harmonious. His interest in religious ideas becomes more marked. He feels doubt and asks that the secret instinct of eternal love may enlighten his soul. Love for everything and everybody becomes the theme of his verse; he sees God in all. His concept of God is not always that of the Christian deity; he was interested in Buddhism but did not accept it absolutely; this interest is most evident in *The Lotus Pool* (1918). *The Constant Beloved* (1920) tells of his one great love. When his beloved dies, he offers his grief to God, for it is all he has to offer.

Nervo said he had no special literary tendency but wrote as he pleased. His only school was his deep perennial sincerity. If he had been rich, he would have written only good verse, but life did not let him write that one "free" volume. His work has appealed to many classes of readers; his name meaning "beloved" was quite suitable.

"If You Are Good," and "The Chestnut Tree" display his mysticism. These poems reveal some pantheism, which is more evident in "Solidarity."

"Why Weep? No More!" was written in 1912 after the death of the woman he loved so dearly. It reveals the poet's deep grief and also his determination not to be overcome by it but rather, to transform it into beauty.

"Thirst," more rhythmical than many of his poems, expresses his unsatisfied yearnings.

"Fill it with Love" might be called a prose poem with a refrain; it has lines of very irregular length and is unrhymed.

LEOPOLDO LUGONES (1874-1938), ARGENTINA

Lugones went to Buenos Aires at the age of twenty. As a correspondent for *La Nación* and with other commissions, he traveled to Europe in 1906, 1911, and 1920. He was very liberal in his views and interested in all kinds of ideas. Besides being a poet, he was an essayist, critic, humanist, and educator, serving as a teacher and supervisor, and Director of the National Council of Education. He was a good friend of Darío when both were clerks in the administrative division of the Post Office Department. Darío tells in his autobiography of the strong impression Lugones made on him through his forceful, bold personality and unusual writings. As he was usually jovial and enthusiastic, his suicide was a surprise to all.

His first volume of verse, *The Mountain of Gold* (1897), was disdained by most critics because of its form and content. Part of the collection was written in unrhymed free verse and printed as prose except that dashes separated the lines. In that work Lugones expounds his idea that a poet is a divinely inspired prophet. "The Garden Twilights" (1905), influenced by Samain, is quite different with its Parnassian technique and frequent ironical tone. The best poems are descriptions of adolescent girls. He introduced some rhymed free verse in this collection. He later developed this type of verse with musical effects. *Sentimental Calendar* (1909) became the "stone of scandal" of modern Argentine poetry. Most of the poems are ironic although some are sentimental. He often uses scientific terms; he justifies this use of seemingly unpoetic words by saying each word conveys a metaphor, for some words have lost their significance through overuse and original ideas demand new forms of expression. He also employs English words occasionally. He says verse can be free of all except rhyme. *Secular Odes* (1910), written on the occasion of the centenary of Argentina's independence, reveals sincere emotion, as he describes the heritage, heroic tradition, and rustic life of Argentina with spontaneity and a realism that has influenced later poets. He finds inspiration in primitive Spanish poetry in his *Collection of Ballads* (1924) and the posthumously published *Ballads of River Seco* (1938), which some consider his greatest work. Many of the poems deal with love although other themes appear, such as the epic civil struggles, legendary subjects, and pictures of customs and types. Although he imitated many writers, he at times surpassed the one imitated. Lugones and Jaimes Freyre disturbed the traditional ideas of rhyme and rhythm; the violence of the opposition is evidence of the importance of their influence.

"The White Solitude" has very striking imagery and is unusual in its metrical form with its verses varying from three to fifteen syllables; it is in assonance. The last two verses contain a personal touch, sadness over the absence of the loved one.

"Twilight Elegy" is in consonantal rhyme and with a regular meter of eleven-syllable verses. It is from the ballad collection and like many ballads, deals with the theme of hopeless love.

JOSÉ SANTOS CHOCANO (1875-1934), PERU

As a child Chocano heard the conquerors' trumpets blow in the victory of Chile over Peru in 1883. He was not trained in humanistic culture and did not study any foreign languages; what foreign literature he knew was from translations, but he did study Spanish and Spanish-American literature. He was imprisoned for taking part in a revolution at the age of nineteen. During his life he traveled over the continent and mixed in politics. He considered Spain lethargic and soon left there, going to Mexico, where he took part in the agrarian revolution. In 1920 while the guest of the president of Guatemala, he was captured and imprisoned by the revolutionists who overthrew the government. Chocano was saved from execution by the plea from friends all over the world not to kill the "poet of America." In Peru he was again accused by political enemies of favoring a tyrannical government, but in spite of this, his friends succeeded in having him crowned national poet of Peru. He was shot to death in a streetcar in Chile.

When Chocano was imprisoned as a youth, he wrote *Holy Anger*, printed in red ink as appropriate to the sentiments expressed in it, lamenting the ills of society and expressing wrath against political iniquity. He feels the poet has a mission to perform to society. *The Epic of the Headland* (1899) praising the patriotism and heroism of the Peruvians in the war with Chile, is a virile sonorous epic. *Fostering America* (1906) reveals his mastery of his art and won him the title of "the poet of America." He includes all Latin America in his vision and acknowledges the spiritual bond with Spain. Darío's poetic prelude recognizes Chocano as spokesman for the continent with his unevenness, tempestuousness, and energy. Chocano feels himself an Inca and a proud American as well as a Spaniard. In one poem, "Epic of the Pacific," he would harmonize Latin imagination, German gravity, and Saxon energy. He is unexcelled in painting the loveliness and warm color of the tropics. He describes the American cities, mountains, rivers, animals, and plants. In *First-Fruits of Gold of the Indies* (1934) he presents the characteristics of the American Indian and is his defender. His poetry is often declamatory but at times is simple and natural and beautiful.

"A Manifesto" is a declaration of poetic principles. Chocano assumes the title of "the poet of autochthonous America," but far from refusing to acknowledge any relationship with Spain, he prides himself on his mixture of Spanish and Indian blood. He feels his multiplicity. If he were not a poet, he would have difficulty in deciding what he would be.

"Who Knows?" reveals deep psychological insight and understanding of the Indian temperament and attitude toward life, as well as awareness of the unjust treatment he has undergone through centuries of oppression. Chocano suggests that his own mixed blood gives him this sympathetic comprehension, and is not sure of what his own reactions would be in certain cases. Although this poem presents a social problem, it also presents a psychological study of the Indian nature, which has learned to compensate for the injustices dealt it.

JULIO HERRERA Y REISSIG (1875-1910), URUGUAY

Although Herrera y Reissig's uncle was once President of Uruguay and his patrician family had been active in politics, Julio disdained political life. As he had poor health, he was allowed to follow his own whims. He read much, liking especially the works of Poe, Baudelaire, Schopenhauer, and Nietzsche. When Darío visited Buenos Aires, Herrera y Reissig became one of his followers. He established his "ivory tower" in a garret that he called "The Tower of the Panoramas." A group of young Moderns frequented this place. As his poems were criticized for their extravagance, he issued a "decree," proclaiming the literary immunity of his person, in such phrases as "I only and by myself" and "I am the emperor." He liked to astonish people. He hated vulgarity in life and in literature and isolated himself from the world. Contracting heart disease, he died in 1910. Although he was ignored by his contemporaries, his reputation has increased greatly as his type of writing came in vogue.

Herrera y Reissig has had great influence on Argentine poets and he has been recognized as the precursor of Creationism. In his complex work he strove for novelty with striking images considered very novel in his life. He was often impressionistic. He wrapped his thought up in nebulosities of thought and language. His melancholy is evident. His irony as he presents the commonplace life of the village is also understanding and compassionate. He often ends a description of a rustic scene with a note of weirdness. Bold images appear unexpectedly as when monks are praying at midnight and a brother advances and bows three times with the head he holds in his hand. He has people appear in his landscapes or appropriates landscape as a background for his people, as Rubino Blanco Fombona suggests. The landscape or objects assume life as when the monastery is personified. Ideas often assume life, as when piety licks like a cow or pride growls like a dog.

"July" may mean the month of July or it may be the poet's given name; one is as applicable as the other. It is a good example of his nebulousness and striking metaphors.

"The Return" illustrates his description of routine scenes of rustic life with a rather sympathetic touch.

ENRIQUE GONZÁLEZ MARTÍNEZ (1871-1952), MEXICO

González Martínez practiced medicine fifteen years in Sinaloa. His medical work interested him in the mystery and significance of human existence and he wrote poetry in his leisure time. In 1911 he went to Mexico City and began an active literary career and in 1920 he founded *México moderno,* a literary journal. He taught for some time and held government positions, including that of Minister Plenipotentiary to various countries. His poetry reveals the man himself with his sense of humor, warm personality, and serenity.

His first work reveals the influence of Gutiérrez Nájera and Othón although he is expressing his own ideas. Later he studied French writers and published a volume of translations of French poetry. *In Silence* (1909) shows distinct advancement in his artistry. He expounds his purpose in writing in one of his poems: he would avoid all that astounds and dazzles ordinary people and refine his soul until he could listen to the silence and see the shadow; he would love himself in himself so that epitomizing his being, heaven and abyss, he could contemplate everything without turning his eyes from himself. In *Hidden Paths* (1911) he has formed his philosophy to a large extent: he will work his field, live his life, hold with a firm hand the lighted lamp above the eternal shadows and abyss, and listen to the vast sublime silence of his own soul. He thus regards himself as a teacher trying to enlighten others; art is no longer sufficient to itself but serves a purpose.

The Death of the Swan (1915) largely accomplished what its title suggests, the death of the Modernist swan, although González Martínez was probably not attacking Darío but wished to wring the neck of only the swan of deceitful plumage, trying to delude with its external grace. From this time on the poet strives to interpret and live the soul of things and the voice of the landscape. He longs to fuse his soul in the spirit of the universe. He once defined his poetry as "translating myself and expressing my inquietude before the contemplation of life."

"Wring the Neck of the Swan" has been interpreted by Pedro Salinas in a masterly manner. He suggests that González Martínez not only repudiates the swan but desires to wring the most admired portion of its being. Thirty-five years before Paul Verlaine had urged wringing the neck of eloquence; the two suggested victims are similar. González Martínez attacks the swan as the most brilliant example of the rhetorical euphuism of Modernism. Darío's own references to the swan had become a mannerism. González Martínez chooses another bird, also mythological. The swan's neck is a sign of interrogation and González Martínez seeks a decipherer of signs and an interpreter of the landscape. He does not wish to kill the swan, but to interpret it. The owl of Pallas Athene is noted for its penetrating vision; it symbolizes intelligence and can see in the mysterious and hidden zones of man's life. It disdains the superficial, encourages temperance, and advises of the dangers of movement and tumult. The owl is the more faithful incarnation of the pure classic spirit. The classicism González Martínez propounds is enclosed in the fifth, sixth, and seventh verses of the poem. He attacks the purely formal and verbal aspects of Modernism, the euphuism and the love for words and rich rhymes. His own classicism is an integrating aspiration toward complete art, expressing the total concept of life, ruled by the intellect.

In "Do You Recall?" the poet discusses the change that has taken place in him. He is no longer engrossed in visible forms and audible sounds, for now he has beheld "the crystal soul of life in its profundity."

"When You Know How to Find a Smile" and "As Sister and Brother" reveal the poet's pantheism as he endows all forms of nature with spiritual life.

"The Impossible Return" is discussed in connection with a poem of López Velarde.

RUBEN DARIO

EL CISNE

Fué en una hora divina para el género humano.
El Cisne antes cantaba sólo para morir.
Cuando se oyó el acento del Cisne wagneriano
fué en medio de una aurora, fué para revivir.

Sobre las tempestades del humano oceano
se oye el canto del Cisne; no se cesa de oír,
dominando el martillo del viejo Thor germano
o las trompas que cantan la espada de Argantir.

¡Oh Cisne! ¡Oh sacro pájaro! Si antes la blanca Helena
del huevo azul de Leda brotó de gracia llena,
siendo de la Hermosura la princesa inmortal,

bajo tus blancas alas la nueva Poesía
concibe en una gloria de luz y de armonía
la Helena eterna y pura que encarna el ideal.

SONATINA

La princesa está triste. . .¿qué tendrá la princesa?
Los suspiros se escapan de su boca de fresa,
que ha perdido la risa, que ha perdido el color.
La princesa está pálida en su silla de oro,
está mudo el teclado de su clave sonoro;
y en un vaso olvidada se desmaya una flor.

El jardín puebla el triunfo de los pavos reales.
Parlanchina, la dueña dice cosas banales,
y vestido de rojo piruetea el bufón.
La princesa no ríe, la princesa no siente;
la princesa persigue por el cielo de Oriente
la libélula vaga de una vaga ilusión.

RUBEN DARIO

THE SWAN

It was a wondrous hour for all humanity.
Before, the swan would sing when death was drawing near.
The hour that Wagner's Swan sent forth its melody
Was just at dawn; it meant that new life would appear.

Prevailing over tempests on the human sea,
The singing of the Swan is heard; we still can hear
It rule the mace of Thor, the Nordic deity,
And trumpets singing of the sword of Argantir.

O Swan! O sacred bird! If Helen, fair of face,
Came forth from Leda's azure egg, replete with grace,
Immortal princess of the Beautiful and Real,

New Poesy conceives beneath your wings of white
Amidst a brilliancy of harmony and light,
Eternal Helen, pure incarnated Ideal.

SONATINA

The princess is so sad. Why is the princess in that mood?
Some sighs escape between her lips, that were strawberry-hued,
That now have lost their laughter, lost their color, every trace.
The princess now is pallid, sitting on her golden chair;
The keys of her sonorous clavichord are silent there;
A flower, now forgotten, faints away within a vase.

The peacocks fill the garden with triumphal grand parade.
Banalities are uttered by the chatter-loving maid;
The jester pirouettes in his red costume, bright and gay.
The princess does not laugh; she has no feeling in the least;
The princess is pursuing through the heavens of the east
The vagrant damsel-fly of vague illusion, far away.

¿Piensa acaso en el príncipe de Golconda o de China,
o en el que ha detenido su carroza argentina
para ver de sus ojos la dulzura de luz,
o en el rey de las islas de las rosas fragantes,
o en el que es soberano de los claros diamantes,
o en el dueño orgulloso de las perlas de Ormuz?

¡Ay! la pobre princesa de la boca de rosa
quiere ser golondrina, quiere ser mariposa,
tener alas ligeras, bajo el cielo volar;
ir al sol por la escala luminosa de un rayo,
saludar a los lirios con los versos de Mayo,
o perderse en el viento sobre el trueno del mar.

Ya no quiere el palacio, ni la rueca de plata,
ni el halcón encantado, ni el bufón escarlata,
ni los cisnes unánimes en el lago de azur.
Y están tristes las flores por la flor de la corte;
los jazmines de Oriente, los nelumbos del Norte,
de Occidente las dalias y las rosas del Sur.

¡Pobrecita princesa de los ojos azules!
Está presa en sus oros, está presa en sus tules,
en la jaula de mármol del palacio real;
el palacio soberbio que vigilan los guardas,
que custodian cien negros con sus cien alabardas,
un lebrel que no duerme y un dragón colosal.

¡Oh, quién fuera hipsipila que dejó la crisálida!
(La princesa está triste. La princesa está pálida.)
¡Oh visión adorada de oro, rosa y marfil!
¡Quién volara a la tierra donde un príncipe existe
(La princesa está pálida. La princesa está triste.)
más brillante que el alba, más hermoso que Abril!

¡Calla, calla, princesa—dice el hada madrina—
en caballo con alas hacia acá se encamina,
en el cinto la espada y en la mano el azor,

Is it China's or Golconda's prince of whom her thoughts may be?
Or he who stopped his carriage, that appeared so silvery,
So he might see the sweetness of the light within her eyes;
Or the monarch of the islands filled with roses of sweet scent;
Or he who is the sovereign of diamonds' dazzlement;
Or he who proudly owns some precious pearls as his great prize?

The poor young princess with the mouth that could with roses vie,
Desires to be a swallow, or to be a butterfly,
To have swift wings, to fly beneath the sky quite rapidly;
To reach the sun, ascending by the ladder of a ray,
Give greetings to the lilies with the poetry of May,
Or lose herself within the wind above the thundering sea.

She does not like the palace, nor the distaff's silveriness,
Nor the enchanted falcon, nor the jester in red dress,
Nor swans that seem all of one mind upon the lake of blue.
The sadness of the court's fair flower makes the rest lament;
The dahlias of the west, the jazmines of the orient,
The northern lotus, and the roses that the south once knew.

Unhappy little princess with the heavenly blue eyes!
A captive in the prison that her tulle and gold comprise;
The marble palace seems to her a dungeon, dark and deep;
That palace so superb in which a constant guard appears,
Protected by a hundred negroes with a hundred spears,
A huge old dragon, and a greyhound never known to sleep.

"Oh would I were a butterfly, from chrysalis just freed!"
(The princess now is sad. The princess now is pale indeed.)
O ivory and rose and golden vision of delight!
"Would I might fly off to the land in which a prince might be,
(The princess now is pale. The princess now is sad to see.)
More beautiful than April and the early dawn, so bright!"

"Oh hush, my princess, hush!" her fairy godmother replies;
"From far away on wingèd horse a happy knight now flies;
He has his sword within his belt, and hand with hawk above;

el feliz caballero que te adora sin verte,
y que llega de lejos, vencedor de la Muerte,
a encenderte los labios con su beso de amor!

LO FATAL

Dichoso el árbol que es apenas sensitivo,
y más la piedra dura, porque ésa ya no siente,
pues no hay dolor más grande que el dolor de ser vivo,
ni mayor pesadumbre que la vida consciente.

Ser, y no saber nada, y ser sin rumbo cierto,
y el temor de haber sido y un futuro terror. . .
y el espanto seguro de estar mañana muerto,
y sufrir por la vida y por la sombra y por

lo que no conocemos y apenas sospechamos,
y la carne que tienta con sus frescos racimos,
y la tumba que aguarda con sus fúnebres ramos,
y no saber adónde vamos,
¡ni de dónde venimos . . .!

VERSOS DE OTONO

Cuando mi pensamiento va hacia ti, se perfuma;
tu mirar es tan dulce, que se torna profundo.
Bajo tus pies desnudos aun hay blancor de espuma,
y en tus labios compendias la alegría del mundo.

El amor pasajero tiene el encanto breve,
y ofrece un igual término para el gozo y la pena.
Hace una hora que un nombre grabé sobre la nieve;
hace un minuto dije mi amor sobre la arena.

Las hojas amarillas caen en la alameda,
en donde vagan tantas parejas amorosas.
Y en la copa de Otoño un vago vino queda
en que han de deshojarse, Primavera, tus rosas.

Before he even sees your face, he gives you adoration;
The conqueror of death, he soon will reach his destination,
To bring a glow upon your lips with his sweet kiss of love."

FATALISM

The tree is fortunate, for it is barely sensitive;
Hard stones are still more fortunate for being feelingless,
For nothing gives more pain than just to be alive can give,
Nor more acute affliction than the life of consciousness.

To be, and yet know nothing, with no certain course ahead,
And fear of having been, and fear of what the future brings,
And ever certain terror of tomorrow being dead;
And suffering because of life, of darkness, and of things

That we are not acquainted with, but just suspect the same;
The flesh that with its fresh ripe clusters brings to us temptation;
The tomb that is awaiting us and funeral wreaths proclaim;
And our not knowing whence we came,
Nor less, our destination!

VERSES OF AUTUMN

Whenever my thoughts turn to you, they take on faint perfume;
Your way of looking is so sweet, your glance becomes profound.
Under your uncovered feet is whiteness of the spume,
And on your lips are all the joys that in the world abound.

A transitory love has brief enchantment to bestow,
And bears an equal end of joy or pain within its hand.
It is an hour since I engraved a name upon the snow;
It is a minute since I told my love upon the sand.

The yellow leaves are falling on the promenade these days,
Where many pairs of lovers are so idly wandering.
And in the cup of Autumn some faint trace of wine still stays,
Within which your fair roses soon must drop their petals, Spring.

RICARDO JAIMES FREYRE

LAS VOCES TRISTES

Por las blancas estepas
se desliza el trineo;
los lejanos aullidos de los lobos
se unen al jadeante resoplar de los perros.

Nieva.
Parece que el espacio se envolviera en un velo,
tachonado de lirios
por las alas del cierzo.

El infinito blanco. . .
sobre el vasto desierto,
flota una vaga sensación de angustia,
de supremo abandono, de profundo y sombrío desaliento.

Un pino solitario
dibújase a lo lejos,
en un fondo de brumas y de nieve,
como un largo esqueleto.

Entre los dos sudarios
de la tierra y el cielo,
avanza en el Naciente
el helado crepúsculo de invierno. . .

RICARDO JAIMES FREYRE

THE SAD VOICES

Across the whitened steppe
The sleigh glides on its way;
The howling of the wolves far in the distance
Joins with the labored breathing of the dogs that pull the sleigh.

It snows.
It seems that space has been enveloped in a veil,
That has been trimmed with lilies
By a sweeping northern gale.

Infinitude of whiteness.
Over desert's vast extent,
There floats a vague sensation of deep anguish,
Supreme abandonment, and somber and profound discouragement.

Afar is silhouetted
A solitary pine,
Against a background formed of mist and snow,
A skeleton's long line.

Between the two white shrouds
That earth and sky unfold,
Advances in the east
The early winter morning, freezing cold.

LO FUGAZ

La rosa temblorosa
se desprendió del tallo,
y la arrastró la brisa
sobre las aguas turbias del pantano.

Una onda fugitiva
le abrió su seno amargo,
y estrechando a la rosa temblorosa
la deshizo en sus brazos.

Flotaron sobre el agua
las hojas como miembros mutilados,
y confundidas con el lodo negro,
negras, aun más que el lodo, se tornaron.

Pero en las noches puras y serenas
se sentía vagar en el espacio
un leve olor de rosa
sobre las aguas turbias del pantano.

FLEETINGNESS

The rose fell from the stem
Where it clung tremblingly,
And breezes wafted it
Above the swamp with its turbidity.

A fleeting wave then opened
Its bitter deep recesses,
And holding in its arms the trembling rose,
Destroyed it with caresses.

The petals floated, seeming
Maimed members lopped from bodies they once knew,
And they, confounded with the blackest mire,
Turned even blacker than the mire in hue.

But on the nights that were serene and pure
One sensed in space there floated vagrantly
A rose's faint aroma
Above the swamp with its turbidity.

AMADO NERVO

SI ERES BUENO

Si eres bueno, sabrás todas las cosas,
sin libros. . .y no habrá para tu espíritu
nada ilógico, nada injusto, nada
negro, en la vastedad del universo.

El problema insoluble de los fines
y las causas primeras,
que ha fatigado a la Filosofía,
será para ti diáfano y sencillo.

El mundo adquirirá para tu mente
una divina transparencia, un claro
sentido, y todo tú serás envuelto
en una inmensa paz. . .

EL CASTANO NO SABE

El castaño no sabe que se llama castaño;
mas al aproximarse la madurez del año
nos da su noble fruto de perfume otoñal;
y Canopo no sabe que Canopo se llama;
pero su orbe coloso nos envía su llama,
y es de los universos el eje sideral.

Nadie mira la rosa que nació en el desierto;
mas ella, ufana, erguida, muestra el cáliz abierto,
cual si mandara un ósculo perenne a la extensión.
Nadie sembró la espiga del borde del camino,
ni nadie la recoge; mas ella, con divino
silencio, dará granos al hambriento gorrión.

¡Cuántos versos ¡oh, cuántos!, pensé que nunca he escrito,
llenos de ansias celestes y de amor infinito,
que carecen de nombre, que ninguno leerá;

AMADO NERVO

IF YOU ARE GOOD

If you are good, you will know everything
Without a book. . . For your spirit there will be
No thing illogical, unjust, or wretched
In the universe's whole immensity.

The problem so unsolvable of ends
And of the first cause too,
That has fatigued philosophy so much
Will be quite simple and quite clear for you.

The world will then acquire within your mind
Clear meaning and divine transparency,
And you will find yourself completely wrapped
In calm serenity.

THE CHESTNUT TREE

The chestnut tree is not aware of what its name may be,
And yet as every passing year draws near maturity,
It gives us autumn perfume that its noble fruits disperse;
The star Canopus does not know Canopus is its name,
And yet as its colossal orb sends us a glow, like flame,
It serves as the sidereal axis of the universe.

Nobody ever contemplates the native desert rose,
And yet it is erect and proud; its open calyx shows
As if it sent perennial kisses to the boundless space.
Nobody ever sowed the wheat that grows along the way;
Nobody ever harvests it, and yet its grain some day
Will feed the hungry sparrow with divinely silent grace.

How many, many verses I have thought but did not write,
Filled with celestial yearnings and with love of holiest height,
That fail to have a title and no one will ever see!

pero que, como el árbol, la espiga, el sol, la rosa,
cumplieron ya, prestando su expresión armoniosa
a la INEFABLE ESENCIA, que es, ha sido y será!

SOLIDARIDAD

Alondra, ¡vamos a cantar!
Cascada, ¡vamos a saltar!
Riachuelo, ¡vamos a correr!
Diamante, ¡vamos a brillar!
Aguila, ¡vamos a volar!
Aurora, ¡vamos a nacer!
¡A cantar!
¡A saltar!
¡A correr!
¡A brillar!
¡A volar!
¡A nacer!

LLORAR? POR QUE!

Éste es el libro de mi dolor:
lágrima a lágrima lo formé;
una vez hecho, te juro, por
Cristo, que nunca más lloraré.
¿Llorar? ¡Por qué!

Serán mis rimas como el rielar
de una luz íntima, que dejaré
en cada verso; pero llorar,
¡eso ya nunca! ¿Por quién? ¿Por qué?

Serán un plácido florilegio
un haz de notas que regaré
y habrá una risa por cada arpegio.
¿Pero una lágrima? ¡Qué sacrilegio!
Eso ya nunca. ¿Por quién? ¿Por qué?

Yet they, just like the chestnut tree and wheat and star and rose,
Fulfilled their mission with the harmony their form bestows
On that INEFFABLE ESSENCE that is, has been, shall be.

SOLIDARITY

Little lark, let us sing a song!
Waterfall, let us leap along!
Rivulet, let us run with mirth!
Diamond, let us be very bright!
Eagle, now let us take our flight!
Dawn of day, let us have new birth!
Sing a song!
Leap along!
Run with mirth!
Be very bright!
Take our flight;
Have new birth!

WHY WEEP? NO MORE!

This is the book of my distressing grief;
I formed it tear on tear from pain I bore;
Now it is made, I swear by my belief
In Christ to weep no longer as before.
Why weep? No more!

My poems now will have the brilliant shining
Of my own inner light that I shall pour
Upon each verse; no weeping and repining!
For whom? And why? Now I shall weep no more!

They will be like a calm anthology,
A sheaf of lovely notes I cause to soar,
And each arpeggio a gay laugh will be.
As for a tear? What sacrilege to see!
For whom? And why? Now I shall weep no more!

LA SED

Inútil la fiebre que aviva tu paso;
no hay fuente que pueda saciar tu ansiedad
por mucho que bebas. . .
El alma es un vaso
que sólo se llena con eternidad.

¡Qué mísero eres! Basta un soplo frío
para helarte. . . Cabes en un ataúd;
¡y en cambio a tus vuelos es corto el vacío,
y la luz muy tarda para tu inquietud!

¿Quién pudo esconderte, misteriosa esencia,
entre las paredes de un vil cráneo? ¿Quién
es el carcelero que con la existencia
te cortó las alas? ¿Por qué tu conciencia,
si es luz de una hora, quiere el sumo BIEN?

Displicente marchas del orto al ocaso;
no hay fuente que pueda saciar tu ansiedad
por mucho que bebas. . . ¡El alma es un vaso
que sólo se llena con eternidad!

THIRST

In vain is the fever that quickens your footsteps;
No fountain can quench the deep longing you know,
Howe'er much you drink. . .
For your soul is a cup
That only eternity can overflow.

How wretched you are! A cold wind is sufficient
To freeze you. . .A casket quite easily holds you!
And yet endless space is too short for your flights,
And light seems delayed as disquiet enfolds you!

Who hid you, the being with mystery fraught,
Within the base cranium's walls? And who clipped
Your wings in the prison existence has brought?
If consciousness comes to light only a day,
Why then is "the greatest good" eagerly sought?

You go discontented now east and now west;
No fountain can quench the deep longing you know,
Howe'er much you drink. . .For your soul is a cup
That only eternity can overflow!

LLENALO DE AMOR

Siempre que haya un hueco en tu vida, llénalo de amor.
Adolescente, joven, viejo: siempre que haya un hueco en tu vida, llénalo de amor.
En cuanto sepas que tienes delante de ti un tiempo baldío, ve a buscar al amor.
No pienses: "Sufriré."
No pienses: "Me engañarán."
No pienses: "Dudaré."
Ve, simplemente, diáfanamente, regocijadamente, en busca del amor.
¿Qué índole de amor? No importa: todo amor está lleno de excelencia y de nobleza.
Ama como puedas, ama a quien puedas, ama todo lo que puedas. . ., pero ama siempre.
No te preocupes de la finalidad de tu amor.
Él lleva en sí mismo su finalidad.
No te juzgues incompleto porque no responden a tus ternuras; el amor lleva en sí su propia plenitud.
Siempre que haya un hueco en tu vida, llénalo de amor.

FILL IT WITH LOVE

Whenever there may be a hollow in your life, fill it with love.
As adolescent, young, or old, when there may be a hollow in your life, fill it with love.
When you discover that you have before you time not planned for any use, then go to seek for love,
Not thinking, "I shall suffer."
Not thinking, "They deceive me."
Not thinking, "I shall doubt."
Go with simplicity, transparently, rejoicingly, in search of love.
What kind of love? It does not matter, for all love is full of excellence and nobleness.
Love howsoever you can; love whomsoever you can; and love all that you can; but always love.
Do not concern yourself about the purpose of your love.
It carries its own purpose in itself.
Do not regard yourself as incomplete because of no response to your affection; love carries its own plenitude within itself.
Whenever there may be a hollow in your life, fill it with love.

LEOPOLDO LUGONES

LA BLANCA SOLEDAD

Bajo la calma del sueño,
calma lunar de luminosa seda,
la noche
como si fuera
el blanco cuerpo del silencio,
dulcemente en la inmensidad se acuesta.
Y desata
su cabellera,
en prodigioso follaje
de alamedas.

Nada vive sino el ojo
del reloj en la torre tétrica,
profundizando inútilmente el infinito
como un agujero abierto en la arena.
El infinito.
Rodado por las ruedas
de los relojes,
como un carro que nunca llega.

La luna cava un blanco abismo
de quietud, en cuya cuenca
las cosas son cadáveres
y las sombras viven como ideas.
Y uno se pasma de lo próxima
que está la muerte en la blancura aquella.
De lo bello que es el mundo
poseído por la antigüedad de la luna llena.
Y el ansia tristísima de ser amado,
en el corazón doloroso tiembla.

Hay una ciudad en el aire,
una ciudad invisible suspensa,
cuyos vagos perfiles
sobre la clara noche transparentan,

LEOPOLDO LUGONES

THE WHITE SOLITUDE

Under tranquillity of sleep,
Lunar tranquillity of luminous silk,
The night
As if it were
The white embodiment of silence,
Quite softly goes to bed in the immensity,
And unbinds
Her lengthy tresses,
In the prodigious foliage
Of poplar groves.

Nothing is living but the eye
Of the clock upon the gloomy tower,
Penetrating uselessly into the infinite
As in a hole left open in the sand.
The infinite,
Rotated by the wheels
Of all the clocks,
Like a cart that never does arrive.

The moon is digging a white chasm
Of quietude, in whose valley
Objects are naught but cadavers
And shadows take on life as the ideas.
And one is then astounded at how near
Death's presence is there in that whiteness.
At how beautiful the world is
When it is possessed by the ancientness of the full moon.
And very melancholy longing to be loved,
Is trembling in the sad and aching heart.

There is a city in the air,
Suspended and almost invisible,
Whose vaporous dim outlines
Appear transparent over the clear night

como las rayas de agua en un pliego,
su cristalización poliédrica.
Una ciudad tan lejana,
que angustia con su absurda presencia.

¿Es una ciudad o un buque
en el que fuésemos abandonando la tierra,
callados y felices,
y con tal pureza,
que sólo nuestras almas
en la blancura plenilunar vivieran?. . .

Y de pronto cruza un vago
estremecimiento por la luz serena.
Las líneas se desvanecen,
la inmensidad cámbiase en blanca piedra,
y sólo permanece en la noche aciaga
la certidumbre de tu ausencia.

Like water-marks upon a sheet of paper,
In polyhedrical crystallization.
A city that so far away,
Brings anguish, being so absurdly present.

Is it a city or a boat
In which we might be going thus abandoning the earth,
Quite happy and in silence,
And with such purity,
That just our souls alone
Would be alive within the full moon's whiteness?

And quite suddenly there crosses
Through the tranquil light a certain agitation.
The boundaries are evanescing,
Immensity is being changed now to white stone,
And all remaining in the melancholy night
Is certainty that you are absent.

ELEGIA CREPUSCLAR

Desamparo remoto de la estrella,
hermano del amor sin esperanza,
cuando el herido corazón no alcanza
sino el consuelo de morir por ella.

Destino a la vez fútil y tremendo
de sentir que con gracia dolorosa
en la fragilidad de cada rosa
hay algo nuestro que se está muriendo.

Ilusión de alcanzar, franca o esquiva,
la compasión que agonizando implora,
en una dicha tan desgarradora
que nos debe matar por excesiva.

Eco de aquella anónima tonada
cuya dulzura sin querer nos hizo
con la propia delicia de su hechizo
un mal tan hondo al alma enajenada.

Tristeza llena de fatal encanto,
en el que ya incapaz de gloria o de arte,
sólo acierto, temblando, a preguntarte
¡qué culpa tengo de quererte tanto!. . .

TWILIGHT ELEGY

Remote forlornness in the star there lies,
Love's brother in whom naught of hope remains,
When all the sorely wounded heart attains
Is consolation that for her he dies.

A fate both futile and quite terrifying
Of feeling that with grace and agony
In every rose's fair fragility
Is something of our own that too is dying.

Illusion that compassion e'er will press
Our suit, in frank or hidden guise entreat,
Gives happiness as rending as complete,
So it might kill us by its great excess.

The echo of that nameless melody,
Whose sweetness without wishing did great harm
With that delight it caused by its own charm,
That filled our souls with greatest ecstasy.

A sadness that some fatal charms imbue,
Where neither art nor glory can inspire,
All I can do is tremblingly inquire
Why I am blamed for dearly loving you!

JOSE SANTOS CHOCANO

BLASON

Soy el cantor de América autóctono y salvaje;
mi lira tiene un alma, mi canto un ideal.
Mi verso no se mece colgado de un ramaje
con un vaivén pausado de hamaca tropical. . .

Cuando me siento Inca, le rindo vasallaje
al Sol, que me da el cetro de su poder real;
cuando me siento hispano y evoco el Coloniaje,
parecen mis estrofas trompetas de cristal. . .

Mi fantasía viene de un abolengo moro:
los Andes son de plata, pero el León de oro;
y las dos castas fundo con épico fragor.

La sangre es española e incaico es el latido;
¡y de no ser Poeta, quizás yo hubiese sido
un blanco Aventurero o un indio Emperador!

—QUIEN SABE!

Indio que asomas a la puerta
de esa tu rústica mansión:
¿para mi sed no tienes agua?
¿para mi frío, cobertor?
¿parco maíz para mi hambre?
¿para mi sueño, mal rincón?
¿breve quietud para mi andanza?. . .
—¡Quién sabe, señor!

Indio que labras con fatiga
tierras que de otros dueños son:
¿ignoras tú que deben tuyas
ser, por tu sangre y tu sudor?
¿ignoras tú que audaz codicia,

JOSE SANTOS CHOCANO

A MANIFESTO

I sing about America in wild and native state;
My lyre possesses soul; my song has ideality.
My verses arc not hanging from a bough to oscillate
Like hammocks of the tropics that are swinging leisurely.

When feeling I am Incan, I revere that potentate,
The Sun, who gives the scepter of his royalty to me!
When Spanish, I invoke the Colonies of later date;
My strophes seem like crystal trumpets with their melody.

My strong imagination comes from Moorish blood of old;
The Andcs are of silver, but Leon is made of gold;
I fuse my races with a sound resembling thunder-claps.

My blood itself is Spanish but is Incan in pulsation;
If I were not a poet, I might have the occupation
Of white adventurer or Incan emperor, perhaps!

WHO KNOWS?

"O Indian there at the door
Of your small dwelling, rude and old,
Do you have water for my thirst?
A cover to protect from cold?
A little corn to give me food?
Some place, though poor, for my repose?
Brief quiet for my wanderings?"
"I may have, sir. Who knows?"

"O Indian who wearily
Tills lands that other owners hold,
Do you not know that blood and sweat
Have made them yours from days of old?
Do you not know bold avarice

siglos atrás, te las quitó?
¿ignoras tú que eres el Amo?
—¡Quién sabe, señor!

Indio de frente taciturna
y de pupilas sin fulgor:
¿qué pensamiento es el que escondes
en tu enigmática expresión?
¿qué es lo que buscas en tu vida?
¿qué es lo que imploras a tu Dios?
¿qué es lo que sueña tu silencio?
—¡Quién sabe, señor!

¡Oh raza antigua y misteriosa,
de impenetrable corazón,
que sin gozar ves la alegría
y sin sufrir ves el dolor:
eres augusta como el Ande,
el Grande Océano y el Sol!
Ése tu gesto que parece
como de vil resignación
es de una sabia indiferencia
y de un orgullo sin rencor.

Corre en mis venas sangre tuya,
y, por tal sangre, si mi Dios
me interrogase qué prefiero
—cruz o laurel, espina o flor,
beso que apague mis suspiros
o hiel que colme mi canción—
responderíale dudando:
—¡Quién sabe, señor!

Took them from you long, long ago?
Do you not know you are the master?"
"It may be, sir. I do not know."

"O Indian with somber brow
And eyes that seem so dull and dead,
What thought does your expression hide
Whose meaning no one ever read?
What are you seeking in your life?
What silent dreams could you disclose?
For what do you beseech your God?"
"Who knows, O sir? Who knows?"

Mysterious and ancient race,
Your hearts are wholly fathomless;
You witness joy without delight
And witness pain without distress;
You are august as are the Andes,
The Sun, and the majestic Sea!
That attitude of yours that seems
As if a base servility
Is one of wise indifference
And pride without vindictiveness.

Your blood is running in my veins,
And that same blood exerts such power
If God should ask which I prefer:
The cross or laurel, thorn or flower,
Some sorrow to enrich my song,
Or kisses to assuage my woes,—
In doubt I should respond to him,
"Who knows, O Lord? Who knows?"

JULIO HERRERA Y REISSIG

JULIO

Flota sobre el esplín de la campaña
una jaqueca sudorosa y fría,
y las ranas celebran en la umbría
una función de ventriloquia extraña.

La Neurastenia gris de la montaña
piensa, por singular telepatía,
con la adusta y claustral monomanía
del convento senil de la Bretaña.

Resolviendo una suma de ilusiones,
como un Jordán de cándidos vellones
la majada eucarística se integra;

y a lo lejos el cuervo pensativo
sueña acaso en un Cosmos abstractivo
como una luna pavorosa y negra.

EL REGRESO

La tierra ofrece el ósculo de un saludo paterno. . .
Pasta un mulo la hierba mísera del camino,
y la montaña luce, al tardo sol de invierno,
como una vieja aldeana, su delantal de lino.

Un cielo bondadoso y un céfiro tierno. . .
La zagala descansa de codos bajo el pino,
y densos los ganados, con paso paulatino,
acuden a la música sacerdotal del cuerno.

Trayendo sobre el hombro leña para la cena,
el pastor, cuya ausencia no dura más de un día,
camina lentamente rumbo de la alquería.

Al verlo la familia le da la enhorabuena. . .
Mientras el perro, en ímpetus de lealtad amena,
describe coleando círculos de alegría.

JULIO HERRERA Y REISSIG

JULY

Above the country's spleen floats dizzily
A megrim with cold perspiration sprayed,
And frogs are celebrating in the shade
A strange ventriloquous activity.

The mountain's thoughts, by strange telepathy,
On which grey neurasthenia has played,
With gloomy claustral mania, are stayed
On a senile convent found in Brittany.

To solve a sum illusions have created,
The eucharistic flock is integrated,
Like a Jordan full of fleeces, white as snow.

Afar the meditative crow, inactive,
Perhaps is dreaming of a world abstractive
As a blackish moon with terrifying glow.

THE RETURN

The earth gives kindly greetings with the kiss that it bestows.
A mule finds scanty forage in the grass along the way,
And in the sluggish winter sunlight now the mountain shows
Her snowy apron, like a village dame in fine array.

The sky is smiling kindly and a gentle zephyr blows.
The shepherdess finds near the pine a restful place to stay;
The cattle, when they hear the hieratic horn, obey
Its music, coming with slow steps in closely crowded rows.

The shepherd, absent for the day from home and family,
Is bearing on his shoulder, wood to cook the meal tonight,
As he walks leisurely until his farmhouse is in sight.

His family receives him with befitting courtesy;
The dog impulsively reveals his willing loyalty,
Describing with his lively tail swift circles of delight.

ENRIQUE GONZALEZ MARTINEZ

TUERCELE EL CUELLO AL CISNE

Tuércele el cuello al cisne de engañoso plumaje
que da su nota blanca al azul de la fuente;
él pasea su gracia no más, pero no siente
el alma de las cosas ni la voz del paisaje.

Huye de toda forma y de todo lenguaje
que no vayan acordes con el ritmo latente
de la vida profunda. . .y adora intensamente
la vida, y que la vida comprenda tu homenaje.

Mira el sapiente buho cómo tiende las alas
desde el Olimpo, deja el regazo de Palas
y posa en aquel árbol el vuelo taciturno. . .

Él no tiene la gracia del cisne, mas su inquieta
pupila que se clava en la sombra, interpreta
el misterioso libro del silencio nocturno.

TE ACUERDAS?

¿Te acuerdas de la tarde en que vieron mis ojos
de la vida profunda el alma de cristal?. . .
Yo amaba solamente los crepúsculos rojos,
las nubes y los campos, la ribera y el mar. . .

Mis ojos eran hechos para formas sensibles;
me embriagaba la línea, adoraba el color;
apartaba mi espíritu de sueños imposibles;
desdeñaba las sombras enemigas del sol.

Del jardín me atraían el jazmín y la rosa,
(la sangre de la rosa, la nieve del jazmín),
sin saber que a mi lado pasaba temblorosa
hablándome en secreto el alma del jardín.

ENRIQUE GONZALEZ MARTINEZ

WRING THE NECK OF THE SWAN

Wring the swan's curved neck; that bird of false display
Bestows its note of whiteness on the fountain's blue;
Though it parades its grace, it never felt or knew
The soul of things, nor heard what nature's voices say.

Avoid all form and language not in every way
In harmony with latent rhythm that must imbue
All life with depth, and let your love for life be true,
And may life comprehend the homage that you pay.

Regard the wise old owl; his wings are widely spread,
To leave Athena on Olympus overhead;
Now resting on that tree, he ends his silent flight.

He lacks the swan's grace, but his eyes that restlessly
Explore the shadows, comprehend all mystery
In that strange volume of the silence of the night.

DO YOU RECALL?

Do you recall the evening that my eyes beheld
The crystal soul of life in its profundity?
I used to love alone the reddish twilight hours,
The meadows and the clouds, the beaches and the sea.

My eyes were made for forms that are perceptible;
A line would give delight, and color always please;
I kept my spirit free from dreams beyond attainment;
I scorned the shadows, as the sun's great enemies.

The garden's sole attractions were the rose and jazmine,
(Because of roses' blood, because of jazmines' snow,)
And though the garden's soul walked trembling at my side,
And talked to me in secret, I would never know.

Halagaban mi oído las voces de las aves,
la balada del viento, el canto del pastor,
y yo formaba coro con las notas suaves,
y enmudecían ellas y enmudecía yo. . .

Jamás seguir lograba el fugitivo rostro
de lo que ya no existe, de lo que ya se fué. . .
Al fenecer la nota, al apagarse el astro,
¡oh, sombras, oh silencio, dormitabais también!

¿Te acuerdas de la tarde en que vieron mis ojos
de la vida profunda el alma de cristal?. . .
Yo amaba solamente los crepúsculos rojos,
las nubes y los campos, la ribera y el mar. . .

CUANDO SEPAS HALLAR UNA SONRISA. . .

Cuando sepas hallar una sonrisa
en la gota sutil que se rezuma
de las porosas piedras, en la bruma,
en el sol, en el ave y en la brisa;

cuando nada a tus ojos quede inerte,
ni informe, ni incoloro, ni lejano,
y penetres la vida y el arcano
del silencio, las sombras y la muerte;

cuando tiendas la vista a los diversos
rumbos del cosmos, y tu esfuerzo propio
sea como potente microscopio
que va hallando invisibles universos;

entonces en las flamas de la hoguera
de un amor infinito y sobrehumano,
como el santo de Asís, dirás hermano
al árbol, al celaje y a la fiera.

Sentirás en la inmensa muchedumbre
de seres y de cosas tu ser mismo;

My ear would be allured by voices of the birds,
By ballads of the wind, and by a shepherd's strain,
And I would form a chorus with the softened notes,
And then they would grow still, and I grew still again.

I was not able to pursue the fleeting face
Of what no longer was, of what had bid adieu.
When notes would die away, and stars would cease to shine,
O shadows, O deep silence, you were dozing too!

Do you recall the evening that my eyes beheld
The crystal soul of life in its profundity?
I used to love alone the reddish twilight hours,
The meadows and the clouds, the beaches and the sea.

WHEN YOU KNOW HOW TO FIND A SMILE

Whenever you have learned to find a smile
Within the tiny water drop that squeezes
Its way through porous stone, within the mist,
Within the sun, within the birds and breezes;

When nothing in your sight remains remote,
Nor formless, nor inert, nor colorless;
And you can penetrate the life and secret
That silence, death, and shadows may possess;

When you extend your sight so that the cosmos
Is brought within your vision more and more,
Your efforts like a mighty microscope
Discovering some worlds not seen before;

Then in the flames of that bright burning fire
Of superhuman love beyond all others,
As Francis of Assisi you will call
Wild beasts and trees and clouds' formations "brothers."

And you will feel the multitude of beings
And things, and your own self are all allied;

serás todo pavor con el abismo
y serás todo orgullo con la cumbre.

Sacudirá tu amor el polvo infecto
que macula el blancor de la azucena,
bendecirás las márgenes de arena
y adorarás el vuelo del insecto:

y besarás el garfio del espino
y el sedeño ropaje de las dalias. . .
Y quitarás piadoso tus sandalias
por no herir a las piedras del camino.

COMO HERMANA Y HERMANO. . .

Como hermana y hermano
vamos los dos cogidos de la mano. . .

En la quietud de la pradera hay una
blanca y radiosa claridad de luna,
y el paisaje nocturno es tan risueño
que con ser realidad parece sueño.
De pronto, en un recodo del camino,
oímos un cantar. . .Parece el trino
de un ave nunca oída,
un canto de otro mundo y de otra vida. . .
¿Oyes?—me dices—. Y a mi rostro juntas
tus pupilas preñadas de preguntas.
La dulce calma de la noche es tanta
que se escuchan latir los corazones.
Yo te digo: no temas, hay canciones
que no sabremos nunca quién las canta. . .

Como hermana y hermano
vamos los dos cogidos de la mano. . .

Besado por el soplo de la brisa,
el estanque cercano se divisa. . .
bañándose en las ondas hay un astro;

With an abyss you too will be all fear,
With soaring heights you too will be all pride.

You will be moved by love for tainted dust
That leaves a stain upon the lily's white;
You will give blessing to the sandy banks;
You will revere the tiny insect's flight.

And you will kiss the thorn tree's spiny hook,
And drapery of the dahlia's silk array;
And will remove your shoes with reverence,
So not to wound the stones along the way.

AS SISTER AND BROTHER

As a sister and a brother,
The two of us are walking, holding hands.

There is within the meadow's quietude
The radiant white brightness of the moon,
And the nocturnal landscape is so smiling
That though reality, it seems a dream.
Abruptly, at a winding of the road,
We hear some singing. . . . It is like the trill
Of a bird not heard before,
A singing from another world and life.
And as you ask me, "Do you hear?" you fix
Your eyes replete with questions on my face.
The atmosphere is so completely calm
That we can hear the beating of our hearts.
I tell you not to fear, for there are songs
That we shall hear but never know who sings them.

As a sister and a brother
The two of us are walking, holding hands.

The pond that is quite near is dimly seen,
Receiving kisses from the breeze's breath.
A star is bathing now within the waves;

un cisne alarga el cuello lentamente
como blanca serpiente
que saliera de un huevo de alabastro.
Mientras miras el agua silenciosa,
como un vuelo fugaz de mariposa
sientes sobre la nuca el cosquilleo,
la pasajera onda de un deseo,
el espasmo sutil, el calosfrío
de un beso ardiente cual si fuera mío.
Alzas a mí tu rostro amedrentado
y trémula murmuras: ¿me has besado?
Tu breve mano oprime
mi mano; y yo a tu oído: ¿sabes? Esos
besos nunca sabrás quién los imprime.
Acaso ni siquiera si son besos.

Como hermana y hermano
vamos los dos cogidos de la mano. . .

En un desfalleciente desvarío
tu rostro apoyas en el pecho mío,
y sientes resbalar sobre tu frente
una lágrima ardiente. . .
Me clavas tus pupilas soñadoras
y tiernamente me preguntas:—¿Lloras?. . .
—Secos están mis ojos. . .Hasta el fondo
puedes mirar en ellos. . .Pero advierte
que hay lágrimas nocturnas—te respondo—
que no sabemos nunca quién las vierte. . .

Como hermana y hermano
vamos los dos cogidos de la mano. . .

A swan extends quite leisurely its neck,
That seems a snow-white serpent
Emerging from an egg of alabaster.
While you are looking at the silent water,
As if a butterfly flew swiftly by,
You have a ticklish feeling on your neck,
The transitory wave of a desire,
The muscle's light contraction, and the shiver
Caused by a kiss, as ardent as if mine.
You look at me with terror-stricken face,
And tremulous, you murmur, "Did you kiss me?"
Your small hand presses mine;
And I say softly, "Do you understand?
You never will know who bestows those kisses.
It may be that they are not even kisses."

As a sister and a brother,
The two of us are walking, holding hands.

Then suffering a languid giddiness,
You must support your face against my breast,
And now you feel there slips along your brow
A tear that seems to burn.
You fix on me your eyes so full of dreams
And ask me tenderly, "Can you be weeping?"
"My eyes are dry . . . You can look into them
Down to the very depths . . . But bear in mind
There are nocturnal tears," I answer you,
"But we do not know who is shedding them."

As a sister and a brother
The two of us are walking, holding hands.

EL RETORNO IMPOSIBLE

Yo sueño con un viaje que nunca emprenderé,
un viaje de retorno, grave y reminiscente. . .

Atrás quedó la fuente
cantarina y jocunda, y aquella tarde fué
esquivo el torpe labio a la dulce corriente.
¡Ah, si tornar pudiera! Mas sé que inútilmente
sueño con ese viaje que nunca emprenderé.

Un pájaro en la fronda cantaba para mí. . .
Ya crucé por la senda de prisa, yo no lo oí.

Un árbol me brindaba su paz. . .A la ventura,
pasé cabe la sombra sin probar su frescura.
Una piedra le dijo a mi dolor: "Descansa,"
y desdeñé las voces de aquella piedra mansa.

Un sol reverberante brillaba para mí;
pero bajé los ojos al suelo, yo no lo ví.

En el follaje espeso
se insinuaba el convite de un ósculo divino. . .
Yo seguí mi camino
y no recibí el beso.

Hay una voz que dice: "Retorna, todavía
el ocaso está lejos; vuelve tu rostro, guía
tus pasos al sendero que rememoras; tente
y refresca tus labios en la sagrada fuente;
ve, descansa al abrigo
de aquel follaje amigo;
oye la serenata del ave melodiosa,
y en la piedra que alivia de cansancios reposa;
ve que la noche tarda
y oculto entre las hojas hay un beso que aguarda. . ."

THE IMPOSSIBLE RETURN

I dream about a journey I shall never try,
One grave and reminiscent, turning back again.

I let the spring remain
Behind, a merry songstress; my stupid lips were shy,
Avoiding that fresh current that evening with disdain.
O would I might return! However all in vain
I dream about that journey I shall never try.

A bird was singing in the leaves as I drew near;
I walked along the path in haste and failed to hear.

A tree would grant its peace, but I quite casually
Passed by and never knew how cool the shade might be.
A stone said to my suffering, "Stay here and rest."
I scorned the graciousness that gentle stone expressed.

A sun was glistening with dazzling light for me,
But I was looking at the ground and failed to see.

Within the leafiness
Were hints inviting to a wondrous kiss one day;
I went along my way,
Receiving no caress.

There is a voice that says, "Return, for even yet
The sun is far from setting; turn around and let
Your feet retrace the pathway you recall; then stay
To taste the coolness of the sacred spring's clear spray.
Go; rest in the protection
Of foliage's affection;
Now hear the bird that serenades in dulcet tone;
Relieve your weariness by resting on that stone.
Now see how night delays,
And hidden by the leaves, a kiss awaiting stays. . ."

Mas ¿para qué, si al fin de la carrera
hay un beso más hondo que me espera,
y una fuente más pura,
y una ave más hermosa que canta en la espesura,
y otra piedra clemente
en que posar mañana la angustia de mi frente,
y un nuevo sol que lanza
desde la altiva cumbre su rayo de esperanza?

Y mi afán repentino
se para vacilante en mitad del camino,
y vuelvo atrás los ojos, y sin saber por qué,
entre lo que recuerdo y entre lo que adivino,
bajo el alucinante misterio vespertino,
sueño con ese viaje que nunca emprenderé.

But why, if at the end of my career
There waits for me a sweeter kiss than here,
A fountain still more pure,
A bird within the woods that sings with more allure,
Another stone as kind,
Whose proffered rest my anguished brow some day may find,
And a new sun to throw
Down from its lofty height a ray of hope below?

My sudden eagerness
Stops midway on the road in hesitant distress;
I turn my glances backward and not knowing why,
Between what I recall and what I only guess,
Within the mystery of dusk's deceptive dress,
I dream about that journey I shall never try.

The Post-Modernists

Delmira Agustini

Alfonsina Storni

Juana de Ibarbourou

Enrique Banchs

Rafael Alberto Arrieta

Rafael Arévalo Martínez

Ramón López Velarde

Jorge Luis Borges

Jaime Torres Bodet

Pablo Neruda

The Post-Modernists

DELMIRA AGUSTINI (1886-1914), URUGUAY

As Delmira Agustini was taught at home, she associated little with other children and later considered young people too frivolous to enjoy their society. She married the handsome son of a wealthy family; he was a horse dealer and not in sympathy with her literary aspirations. She soon returned home and filed suit for separation. Although the circumstances are not clear, he evidently killed her, when she later met him secretly, and then committed suicide. Her life has often been compared to a fire, a meteor, or lightning flash because of its brevity, intensity, and glow.

Dr. Sidonia Carmen Rosenbaum calls Delmira's *The White Book* (1907) the white phase of her love, with its purity although it may be considered blue for dreams; or rose, for optimism. It includes her favorite themes—her muse, mystery, development of a great race, and love. *Morning Songs* (1910) shows greater maturity of thought; in one poem, "The Miraculous Boat," the great rhythm of a bloody heart of superhuman life will move her beautiful ship as it sails without a course. In 1913 she reprinted some of these earlier poems and added others in *The Empty Chalices,* which is offered to Eros; thus she enters the "red phase," mentioned by Dr. Rosenbaum, with her frank expression of her most intimate yearnings. She speaks of the physical aspects of love. Middle class society was shocked by this volume and the ladies avoided her.

Her posthumous works reveal even more intense passion. She combines the three primary poetic themes of life, love, and death; they are often presented as visions or dreams. She yearns for an impossible love and a superhuman life; she longs to grasp the unattainable. Neruda later expresses similar aspirations.

Alberto Zum Felde has noted Nietzche's influence on Delmira's theme of a superhuman race. Herrera y Reissig also seems to have influenced her. She became the inspiration of other Spanish-American poetesses who strove to express their own originality. Some acknowledged her influence as Juana de Ibarbourou did when she called her the "lay saint" and "older sister" of these women.

"The Intruder," a sonnet with fourteen-syllable lines, is an exaltation of love.

"Your Love" mentions love as concerned with life and death. The figures of speech are characteristic of the poetess' love of contrasts and combines the sensation of pain with pleasure. "Pale Evening" also contains the admission that remembrance of past sadness may have an exquisite taste. She repeats the last word or phrase of the first verse in the last one of each stanza, giving the effect of an echo.

"The Wings" suggests her longing for something beyond this world; in this poem human love seems to have caused the loss of her wings that carried her on flights to superhuman situations.

"Nocturne" is a beautiful fantasy.

ALFONSINA STORNI (1892-1938), ARGENTINA

Alfonsina Storni was born in Switzerland but was reared in Argentina. As her family was poor, she was compelled to earn her own living quite young, joining an itinerant theatrical company. After graduating from a normal school she went to Buenos Aires. Not liking the commercial work she undertook, she turned to teaching and assisting in an experimental theater for children, for which she wrote plays. She expressed her sorrows, love, and ideals in her verse. She ended her sad life by leaping into the sea in 1938. She frequently associated the idea of death with the sea; the sea meant liberation, space, infinity.

The Inquietude of the Rosebush (1916) reveals the fearless soul who ignoring tradition and criticism, freely expresses her emotions and thoughts in writing and attends gatherings of men writers. She thus prepared the way for other Argentine women of letters. *The Sweet Torture* (1918) finds no happiness in the present, and its last part reveals a defiant, ironic mood. She longs at times for death and wishes she could not feel. She resents the double code of morals and also begins to interpret the loneliness, vulgarity, and monotonous unification of city life. The colophon of *Irremediably* (1919) states that it was written in two months midst great spiritual stress. The poetess is recalling humble, passionate, amorous moments and also bitter, sylvan, tempestuous ones. *Languidness* (1920) is dedicated to those who like her have never fulfilled a single dream; she decides to abandon subjective poetry which has exhausted all her soul has to say of itself. *Ocher* (1925) introduces the new literary phase, conscious of form and style; she is more ironic and cynical, taking with indifference whatever life gives her. She characterizes *Poems of Love* (1926) as one of so many tears fallen from human eyes.

World of Seven Wells (1934) marks a new phase with its polished form; she does not employ rhyme and she attempts free verse; she uses many images. The most common themes are death and the city.

Each succeeding book becomes more bitter till her last book *Death-Mask and Clover* (1938), composed of antisonnets of fourteen unrhymed lines. In her explanation she says that the key to this new literary trend is found in her fundamental psychic changes, and not in external currents. The reader must offer his imaginative collaboration. She wrote these poems rapidly, almost in a state of trance, in bed, riding, or in public, but polished them during a period of months. She looks into the world beyond that harbors unspoken thoughts and visions that become potently real. She sees strange images but they have sense and logic in that world. She analyzes small details as a tear or a pencil, "a micro-world," full of compressed thought not always easily understood.

Dr. Rosenbaum calls her the only major poetess to carry the feminist banner, portraying the bitterness of women's lot, the injustice of the double standard, and her own rebellion against convention that had kept women from revealing the surging sea within them. This critic goes on to say that she is also feminine, disclosing meekness and submission to the sweet torture of love that she desires.

"Squares and Angles" depicts the poetess' boredom due to the monotony and unification of city life and the stolidity of the people. The repetition of phrases is very appropriate in suggesting that monotony which is affecting her too.

"Dear Little Man," "The One Who Understands," and "Ancestral Weight" reveal directly or indirectly her feminist ideas. "The One Who Understands," with its long lines suggesting heaviness, presents in a very subtle manner the bitterness of woman's lot. "Ancestral Weight" also is subtle in its implications.

"Pain" with its couplets of eleven-syllable lines, with one single consonantal rhyme used for all the stanzas, gives the effect of meditation and dignity. Alfonsina's longing for insensibility to pain or any emotion reminds one of Darío's "Fatalism"; it seems evident, however, that her greatest longing is to be indifferent to men.

JUANA DE IBARBOUROU (1895-   ), URUGUAY

Juana de Ibarbourou, perhaps the most beloved Spanish-American poetess, spent her childhood and adolescence amidst rustic surroundings, which left their imprint on her life and poetry. She married an army officer at the age of eighteen and has led an uneventful life as a wife and mother. She was given the honorary title of "Juana of America" in 1928. She has been described as a beautiful woman radiating goodness and charm.

Her first sonnets published in a newspaper were well received, and her first collection of poems, *Diamond Tongues,* was published in 1919. These poems treat of love in all its forms and created a sensation, although not as great as Delmira Agustini's works caused. Some criticized her unusual frankness and others praised it; her new note of love as a manifestation of nature was copied by many poetesses. She offers herself with naturalness and "chaste impudicity," ignoring the conventions. She feels a deep sympathy with nature and identifies herself with flowers, fruits, insects, and other creatures. Her overflowing vitality is naturally accompanied by a dread of darkness and immobility—death. Her prose collection, *The Fresh Pitcher* (1920) shows her remarkably changed into a serious woman and mother, as she looks back on her childhood and adolescence. *The Wild Root* (1922) has been called the verse commentary on the prose collection. She is sated with this civilized life and longs to be free and happy; although she may flower in roses, no one can change her "savage root." This collection is more tranquil in spirit than the first and more perfect in form with a variety of meters. She looks with longing on past joys and turns to nature for strength; the river can teach her soul to form a backwater. Her horror of death is lessened by the belief that her spirit will live in the various aspects of nature. Meanwhile she speaks of physical love as one aspect of nature, as all nature breathes love.

In *The Rose of the Winds* (1930) she is much more concerned with her style of writing, using many figures of speech; she is in a sadder mood, although she strives to be gay, saying, "I will dance upon my wounded heart." This collection is more obscure. As the prestige of Modernism was declining when she began to write, her verse lacks the exquisite luxury and musical sonority of the Rubén Darío epoch. She has also written children's tales and cradle songs, two textbooks on pedagogy, and poetic prose commentaries of the Litany. Juana is the most feminine of the major Spanish-American poetesses.

"Clinging to Life" and "Fleeting Restlessness" might be considered as the two sides of a coin. In the former the poetess feels that after her death her body will strive to return to this life to enjoy nature and see her lover. Zum Felde calls this poem an "intense cry of longing for life—the most poetic and pathetic image in the materialistic conception of the world." In "Fleeting Restlessness" Juana beseeches her lover to permit her to enjoy nature and life as one day she will be dead.

"Dejection" expresses a pathetic attempt to disguise her sadness and unrest.

"Woman" sounds a similar note to Alfonsina Storni's, but instead of emphasizing the injustices men suffer, Juana envies men's freedom to wander and thus enjoy life.

ENRIQUE BANCHS (1888-), ARGENTINA

Banchs was born in Buenos Aires. He wrote his first book at nineteen years of age and continued to write a great deal up to 1911, but after that time he has written little, although his first works were succesful. Henríquez Ureña said Banchs gave *La Prensa* four sonnets in 1928 that showed his accustomed mastery of form but with romantic emotion. At that time he was editing a page for children in that newspaper.

Unlike many poets Banchs prefers simple themes and emotions, and his style is simple and direct, in contrast to the Modernist poets. He does not strive for unusual metrical effects. He turned to the old ballads for inspiration in *The Book of Eulogies* (1908) and even used archaisms to good effect and in a natural manner as he was able to enter into the spirit of the period he was invoking. His imitation of the repetition of words and phrases characteristic of some ballads is unusually effective, although monotonous at times. He does not always use the same assonance throughout the poem as in the old ballads; the change in assonance gives a pleasing variety. *The Falcon's Bell* (1909) which contains "Stammering," "The Vow," and "A Little Song" also has *La estatua*, a group of four sonnets with the theme of Darío's "Fatalism;" he wishes he might be as unmoved before fate as the beautiful statue he describes. "The Tiger" appears in *The Urn* (1911).

"Stammering" exemplifies Banchs' repetition of phrases and lines, which is natural in this case as if imitating the stammering, hesitant speech of one finding it difficult to express his deep emotion. Consonantal rhyme or repetition of the same word occurs in the even lines.

"A Little Song" has the characteristics of a little song with its six-syllable verses with consonantal rhyme in the even lines and the last word of the first line repeated as the last word of the third line of each stanza except the last, when the two words are reversed in order. The beloved is addressed as if she were a flower in the first three stanzas and as a bird in the last three.

"The Vow," in fourteen-syllable verses with consonantal rhyme, sounds as if a different poet had written it. The theme is also quite different. The poet shows great skill in composing a pleasing poem out of a carpenter's tools and equipment and the articles constructed. Banchs seems to feel that the carpenter can be as artistic and creative in his work as the poet.

"The Tiger" bears additional evidence of the poet's versatility, not only in the sonnet form, but also in the diction and the unexpected ending, turning the objective description of the animal into a subjective matter.

RAFAEL ALBERTO ARRIETA (1889-), ARGENTINA

Arrieta was born in the province of Buenos Aires and has always lived there. He has been a professor of European Literature in the University of La Plata and has won prizes for literary and bibliographical work. He has edited the review *Ateneo* and has collaborated on other literary reviews and on *La Prensa.* He is well acquainted with foreign literature and has translated some of the works of Shakespeare and of Shelley, with whom he seems to be a kindred spirit.

His first work, *The Soul and the Moment* (1910), is representative of his poetry; he seizes and fixes the most fleeting aspect of reality, as exemplified in a later poem, "Mile-Stone," in which a rose causes him to stop and forget the road he has traversed; after describing its effect on him, the poet wonders whether he is dying or being reborn in this sea of forgetfulness. He prefers humble daily themes and traditional meters and makes no display of form; his moderation and serenity lend a classic tone to his work, which, however, is not lacking in sentiment. His collection *Captive Time* (1947) contains fourteen poems dealing with children and the hour before they fall asleep or after they are asleep. The group entitled *Return* are suggestive of lost happiness.

"The Absent Voice" is unique in its use of the refrain. It is set aside in parentheses four times as if the exile were striving not to express his deepest longing, but in the last stanza it appears twice as his love demands expression.

"In an Abandoned Cemetery" is appropriately written in long verses in blank verse, as the poet meditates on the community of human experiences; the realization of the brevity of life enhances his awareness of the beauty of nature, the joy of living, and his happiness in the love of his wife.

RAFAEL ARÉVALO MARTÍNEZ (1884-), GUATEMALA

Rafael Arévalo Martínez is the Director of the National Library of Guatemala and the Honorary President of the Inter-American Bibliographical and Library Association and has been Secretary of the International Central American Bureau and President of the Ateneo of Guatemala. He is the creator of a type of short story known at the psychozoological tale, in which various animals and birds have their human counterpart, as the man who seemed a horse. Although his first poems won fame, he has always striven to improve on his work. He does not belong to any literary school and does not try to employ unusual technique or strive for verbal perfection. He accepts tradition and builds on it, adding his own individuality. He has a message and expresses it. He loves restrained emotion and the correct word. He disdains chiseled pure verse. One critic says he is almost an unliterary poet.

He resembles St. Teresa in his dual nature; at times he is an ardent mystic, at other times he is concerned with the ordinary situations of life. He is like St. Francis of Assisi in his love for all creatures. He describes the nature of love and ends by saying that all love is joy. He proclaims the unity of all things—nettles, thistles, brambles; they are only pieces of one Soul, that is in all things. *Along a Little Road* (1947) contains philosophical poems and some dealing with people's moral obligations and attitude toward life.

"The Men-Wolves," which exemplifies the poet's psychozoological interests, reveals his sympathetic understanding of people's weaknesses and suggests that he himself has similar failings.

"Like the Cypresses" denotes an unwillingness or inability to express his deepest emotions.

RAMÓN LÓPEZ VELARDE (1888-1921), MEXICO

López Velarde was born in the state of Zacatecas. After receiving his law degree in 1912, he held a position as a judge; but not satisfied with that, he went to Mexico City where he held a minor bureaucratic position and worked on an obscure newspaper which published his first poems. Although he was always interested in women, he never married. His amorous desires and inclination toward paganism were in conflict with his love of provincial life, chastity, and Catholicism; he considered himself a frustrated sacristan. This conflict finds expression in his intensely subjective poetry, although many of his followers were conscious only of his use of provincial themes and his striving for effect. His death from pneumonia terminated a promising career as a poet. After his death he became highly esteemed and has had great influence on later poets. He himself seems to have been influenced little by contemporary poets.

In *The Devout Blood* (1916) he believes in the possibility of satisfying himself with the innocent simple love of provincial girls and scorns the more complex and disturbing pleasures of the city. He is preoccupied with death in his last poems; he sees in it the destruction of his flesh. Some of his devices are combining two common elements not usually related, as José Luis Martínez points out. At times he uses a more complex device, using free association, and without developing the suggested image; each phrase includes a new element, and each turn of speech, a verbal find. His metaphors are evidence of his intellect and propensity to verbal audacity. He uses sense images, sometimes combining odor and acoustic and visual images in one metaphor. His abstract allusion may be expressed by the acoustics of words, as when he uses a series of words with scarcely any vowels but *a* and ends by comparing his beloved to "*a* heaped with gifts." He prefers technical to common words, as the Modernists do.

In *The Sound of the Heart* his descriptions are often unintelligible to the uninitiated. His philosophy is disillusioned and bitter.

"The Maleficent Return" has the same theme as "The Impossible Return" of González Martínez. Both poets would like to return to familiar places and long for them. López Velarde, however, dwells on the details of his former surroundings, a "paradise in ruins," with deep longing although he states it is best not to return because he will find his hopes all destroyed. González Martínez stresses certain moments in the past when he did not take advantage of circumstances; although he would like to relive those moments and still thinks of them, he asserts that he will not return and feels that the future may hold moments as good or better. López Velarde employs repetition as the words *new, love, pairs,* and *some.*

JORGE LUIS BORGES (1899-), ARGENTINA

Jorge Luis Borges was born in Buenos Aires but was educated in Switzerland during the first World War. Later he lived in Spain for three years, where he was associated with the Ultraist movement. Returning to Buenos Aires in 1921, he interested the young writers in seeking new forms of expression. He was one of the founders of the reviews *Prisma* and *Proa* and collaborated on the *Índice de la nueva poesía americana.* He has translated Virginia Woolf, Franz Kafka, André Gide, and William Faulkner. He has won various literary prizes and became a scenario writer and producer in 1946.

He decries "Rubenismo" with its turning to Europe for its inspiration and melancholy and believes that ordinary daily life can provide the poet with the best themes. Discarding rhyme, he uses free verse with either short lines and traditional rhythms or those of his own invention. Although some of his lines are musical, he does not consider rhythm the essential quality. He says in the introduction to the *Indice,* "The image is our universal countersign."

In *Fervor of Buenos Aires* (1923) he explains that he is trying to render the tribute of his devotion to the shady and silent corners of the city that retains some incense from the colonial epoch. In explanation of his poetic creed, he intends to oppose the brilliant lyricism bequeathed by Góngora. He wishes to use words in their proverbial acceptation. Borges' book includes some poems made by stringing images together, but some poems are of classic simplicity, and some are full of sentiment.

He is something of a professor and philosopher, as shown in *Inquiries* (1925), in which he analyzes poetry, discusses various types of metaphors, and studies the style and concepts of ancient and modern writers.

The Moon Facing Us printed in large lapidary letters on large square pages, has little rhyme. He explains the title, saying that "Facing Us" makes the moon sociable and belonging to everybody, domesticated, and full of intimacy. He feels the streets and houses as something human and tender with souls, and capable of eternity; the patios are hearts. In the prologue Borges establishes a mystic relation between Buenos Aires and the true realities of things. He sets forth the aspects that have profound reality in him. He feels his poverty in comparison with the magnificent reality of nature and life. In the last poem he says, "So I am returning to God some pennies from the large sum of money He placed in my hands." He stresses the provincial aspects of Buenos Aires, and he likes to use peculiarities of the Creole speeech. The pampa is in his heart and he invokes it frequently. It has an air of melancholy and gives the sensation of the desert.

"The Guitar" and "A Patio" are in free verse with lines of irregular length, varying from three to fifteen syllables in "A Patio." The imagery is important in both poems. In "A Patio" the poet finds poetic value in common things. "The Guitar" is an expression of the poet's great interest in the pampa, which is appropriately evoked by the music. A more personal touch is added in the reference to "her" whose memory is associated with music.

JAIME TORRES BODET (1902-), MEXICO

Torres Bodet was born in Mexico City; his mother was of French descent. He was educated in the National University. After several years of teaching French literature, he entered the diplomatic service, serving in various countries. After returning to Mexico, he held government positions. He took part in the "each-one-teach-one" campaign against illiteracy. He has taken an active part in the United Nations and was director of UNESCO but resigned that post. He has revealed talent in the fields of the novel and essay as well as of poetry.

His verse shows a gradual development from the traditional themes and forms of the Post-Modernist movement to the present, although he has not imitated the exaggerated forms of any group of writers. He is probably describing his own early experiences in the poem "Crypt" in which he depicts himself as seeking his own voice in a labyrinth of mirrors. He seeks himself in the smooth wall of silver but does not find himself. Someone is imprisoned in the labyrinth whom he imitates; so he does not notice his own accent, which sounds amidst all the echoes. He has been associated with the Ulysses group always in close touch with modern French writers. Unlike some contemporary writers he expresses some sentiments and emotions as well as presenting some beautiful images; his verse is also musical.

"Echo" and "Music" are typical of Torres Bodet's musical rhythm, his choice of words with liquid consonants, and his pleasing imagery.

PABLO NERUDA (1904-), CHILE

Pablo Neruda is the pseudonym of Neftali Ricardo Reyes, considered one of the most gifted of contemporary Spanish-American poets. His residence near the sea in his youth has caused him to use the sea motif frequently in his poems. When he went to Santiago to study, carrying a notebook of his verse under his arm, he looked troubled and melancholy. He wrote for reviews while continuing his studies; he was criticized by some and applauded by others because of the strangeness of his poetry. Entering early upon a diplomatic career, he has served in Madrid, Calcutta, Rangoon, and Mexico.

Festival Song (1921) expresses the ardent spirit of renovation in Chile, initiated by the Federation of Students in 1920 and continued by various organizations and institutions. *Twilight* (1923) reveals a great poet; his simple poems are filled with harsh melancholy. In some he recalls the past with nostalgia; others express mad passion and sensual pantheism. *Twenty Poems of Love* (1924) give evidence of his artistic development, due to his new contacts and experiences in the city and his readings, including Walt Whitman's works. These poems dealing with carnal love contain striking images, such as woman being a butterfly of dreams, a lullaby, a gray beret, the voice of a bird, the sky seen from a ship, and a blue hyacinth. *The Enthusiastic Slinger*, written about 1924 but published in 1933, is so named because he speaks of revolving his arms like two mad wings of a windmill and hurling from his heart full of frozen weeping the stones that proclaim him, trying to open a door in the wall that confines, and to splinter the stars; the only result is that the stones return and wound him. Some poems are written without punctuation and in irregular stanzas of from four to twenty-six syllables. Young poets were influenced by this work although the general public was not impressed by its originality. When he was consul in various oriental countries, he sent poems to Spanish-American reviews showing a return to thematic poetry. Those of the first volume of *Residence on the Earth* were written between 1925 and 1935. Arturo Aldunate Phillips says Neruda has captured the awakening of the spiritual desire for liberty and the search for the inner vibration of matter. He uses material aspects of life, apparently insignificant; all his suggested description is formed by those small details. One finds tragedy and pain and deep sentiment in his verse. He awakens visions and states of the soul impossible to describe directly. In his later verse he has descended to human misery and the spirit of the epoch, becoming more universal. In *Spain in the Heart* (1936-1937) he deals with the civil war in Spain and expresses his love and admiration for that country as he laments her suffering. His poetry has become much more realistic, and this phase is continued in *Last Poems* (1937-1944) which includes songs to Stalingrad, indicative of his Communistic leanings. "Canto General de Chile" in *Canto General* (c1950) praises his native land.

Amado Alonso calls Neruda's poetry an eruptive process. His objective constructions are comprehensible and coherent only when regarded from their root of sentiment; thus he is related to Expressionists. Although he seems to disregard all rules, he has certain peculiar practices, such as presenting the inanimate as active, the generic as particular, the abstract as concrete, the subjective as objective and vice versa. He uses certain insistent symbols, but not with their traditional significance. He piles up dissociated members and heterogeneous objects. He feels the radical solitude of man and his anguished uncertainty before his mere existence, surrounded by a ring of extraneous things. He tends to use cosmic, oceanic, or telluric imagery. His poems have a dream quality, as of superimposed photographs. He uses various meters and much free verse. Although he breaks all formal laws of meter, there is a rhythm in his works. Each line of free verse is an emotional unit and each plays a role in the development of the whole stanza. Short lines interspersed provide a rhythm. The long lines represent high points of emotion, accelerating the movement; the short provide rests. The syntactic peculiarities in *Residence on the Earth* are due to his aesthetic ideas about the function of form in poetry and his disintegrating vision of the world and life. He pays greater attention to form in the second volume.

"Bridges" has characteristics of Neruda's later work; he makes the objective subjective, and he makes use of lists; he feels anguish before life itself.

"Walking Around" is a good example of Neruda's use of enumeration. Amado Alonso analyzes the enumeration of places the poet does not want to see as representing senseless movement; he wishes to reside in simple, secure, and primordial matter, such as stones, quiet in themselves and containing valuable matter accumulated through the passage of time. Establishments are prisons man constructs around himself. Notaries represent man's failures and mistakes in life since they center their existence in rigorous regimentation of life, a negation of poetry. He enumerates the ugly things connected with the organized life of man. He goes on amidst all the organization through the offices where men are enslaved and through homes which limit them where the dirty vulgarity of life is displayed in the garments hung to dry in patios, weeping "slow dirty tears." The "water of origins and ashes on which he wanders like a felt swan" represent birth and death.

"Barcarolle" exemplifies what Amado Alonso calls "variations of a theme": the repetition of an element in varied rhythmic combinations. In this poem he uses the phrase "some one would come" twice, the first time with "perhaps"; then at the end of the stanza twice without "perhaps"; the next stanza begins with that phrase as a starting point of a new movement.

DELMIRA AGUSTINI

EL INTRUSO

Amor, la noche estaba trágica y sollozante
cuando tu llave de oro cantó en mi cerradura;
luego, la puerta abierta sobre la sombra helante,
tu forma fué una mancha de luz y de blancura.

Todo aquí lo alumbraron tus ojos de diamante;
bebieron en mi copa tus labios de frescura,
y descansó en mi almohada tu cabeza fragante;
me encantó tu descaro y adoré tu locura.

Y hoy río si tú ríes, y canto si tú cantas;
y si tú duermes, duermo como un perro a tus plantas.
Hoy llevo hasta en mi sombra tu olor de primavera;

y tiemblo si tu mano toca la cerradura,
¡y bendigo la noche sollozante y oscura
que floreció en mi vida tu boca tempranera!

TU AMOR. . .

Tu amor, esclavo, es como un sol muy fuerte:
jardinero de oro de la vida,
jardinero de fuego de la muerte,
en el carmen fecundo de mi vida.

Pico de cuervo con olor de rosas,
aguijón enmelado de delicias
tu lengua es. Tus manos misteriosas
son garras enguantadas de caricias.

Tus ojos son mis medianoches crueles,
panales negros de malditas mieles
que se desangran en mi acerbidad;

crisálida de un vuelo del futuro,
es tu abrazo magnífico y oscuro
torre embrujada de mi soledad.

DELMIRA AGUSTINI

THE INTRUDER

O love, it was upon a tragic sobbing night,
That I heard singing in my lock your golden key;
Then when the door was opened, you appeared to be
Midst startling black a spot of whiteness and of light.

Your eyes like diamonds made everything seem bright;
Your lips of freshness drank of my own cup with me,
Your head laid on my pillow its soft fragrancy;
Your boldness charmed me and your madness gave delight.

Now I laugh when you laugh and sing along with you;
If you sleep, I too sleep at your feet, as dogs would do.
My shadow even, now has your perfume of spring;

I tremble if you touch the lock upon my door,
And bless that gloomy sobbing night forevermore
Your early entrance brought my life its blossoming!

YOUR LOVE

Slavish love for you is like a sun that's bright;
You are the gardener that tends the gold of life;
You are the gardener of death's own fiery light,
Dwelling in the fruitful villa of my life.

Beak of raven with the fragrance of a rose,
Stinger of a bee that pleasures' honey dresses,
So your tongue is. Your mysterious hands disclose
They are claws encased in gauntlets of caresses.

Midnights of my deep affliction are your eyes,
Honeycombs of black where cursed honey lies,
Dripping endlessly upon my bitter mood.

Chrysalis of flight into a future place,
Your magnificent and vaguely felt embrace,
The bewitched tower of my solitude.

TARDE PALIDA

Evocadora el alma palidece
toda velada de un color muy vago,
en el cielo lechoso hay un amago
de tempestad, la tarde palidece.

Enmascarado y lento el sol de Otoño
hacia un poniente turbio se encamina,
sobre el paisaje soñador se inclina,
suave y profundo, del exangüe Otoño

la triste tenaz . . . Yo que en la pálida
floresta del dolor junto a mis rosas,
sé que no aroman nunca más gloriosas
que del Otoño en una tarde pálida.

Como voces lejanas en la noche
vienen al alma los dolores viejos,
cada racha que pasa trae de lejos
otro dolor y otro dolor . . . La noche

vendrá a borrar la tarde blanquecina,
el cielo será un piélago de sombras. . .
¿Alma, de qué te asombras?
¿Crees eterna la tarde blanquecina?

Sí, y tú la amabas ya, ¿verdad? la amabas,
tal llega a amarse un gran dolor amigo,
hermano aciago, trágico testigo
de largos años. . . Alma, tú la amabas

como al gran vaso raro y exquisito
en que apuraras néctares añejos
—el rancio zumo de los males viejos
tiene un sabor de pátina exquisito.—

Pero el sol cae, cae allá a lo lejos
lento y soberbio, como un rey vencido,

PALE EVENING

The soul, evocative in mood, turns pale,
Enveloped in a veil of tribulation,
And in the milky sky is indication
Of tempest; evening is becoming pale.

Bemasked and leisurely the sun of autumn
Goes on its journey toward a troubled west;
Above the dreaming countryside will rest
Tenacious sadness of pale, languid autumn

Profoundly, softly. . .Walking in the pallid,
Wan garden of my grief beside my roses,
I know the sweetest fragrancy reposes
On them on autumn evenings that are pallid.

Like distant voices sounding in the night,
There come upon the soul departed woes,
And from afar, each gust of wind that blows
Brings forth one sorrow, then another. . .Night

Will soon arrive to blot out whitish evening;
The sky itself will be a mass of shade. . .
O soul, why be astounded and afraid?
Will there not be an end to whitish evening?

Oh, yes. Did you not love it once? You loved it,
As one may come to love great friendly pain,
Unhappy brother, that may still remain
As tragic witness of long years. . . You loved it

Just as you loved the goblet, rare and exquisite,
From which you drained the nectars age distills;
The rancid juices left from former ills
Take from the patina a taste quite exquisite.

But now the sun descends there in the distance
Like a conquered king, with slowness and great pride,

en púrpuras ardientes.—Ya ha caído. . .
y en ti perduran los amargos dejos
de un gran pasado triste revivido
en una tarde que murió allá lejos!

LAS ALAS

Yo tenía. . .
¡dos alas!. . .
Dos alas
que del Azur vivían como dos siderales
raíces. . .
Dos alas,
con todos los milagros de la vida, la muerte
y la ilusión. Dos alas,
fulmíneas
como el velamen de una estrella en fuga;
dos alas,
como dos firmamentos
con tormentas, con calmas y con astros. . .

¿Te acuerdas de la gloria de mis alas?. . .
El áureo campaneo
del ritmo, el inefable
matiz atesorando
el Iris todo, mas un Iris nuevo
ofuscante y divino,
que adorarán las plenas pupilas del Futuro
(¡las pupilas maduras a toda luz!) . . .el vuelo. . .

El vuelo ardiente, devorante y único,
que largo tiempo atormentó los cielos,
despertó soles, bólidos, tormentas,
abrillantó los rayos y los astros;
y la amplitud: tenían
calor y sombra para todo el Mundo,
y hasta incubar un *más allá* pudieron.

In glowing purples.—Now its light has died.
The bitter aftertaste remains for you
Of great past sadness that you lived anew
In evening as it died there in the distance.

THE WINGS

I once possessed. . .
Two wings!
Two wings
That were existing as if two sidereal bases
Of the Blue.
Two wings
With all the miracles of life itself, of death,
And of illusion. Two wings
As flashing
As flying sails of some bright star in flight;
Two wings
As if two firmaments
With tempests, times of calm, and heavenly bodies.

Do you recall the glory of my wings?
Their golden harmony
Of rhythm, their ineffable
Bright hues imbued with all the treasure
Held by the Rainbow, but a Rainbow new,
And dazzling, and divine,
That will be worshipped by the Future's perfect eyes,
(The eyes that have perception of all light!). . . the flight.

The ardent, ravenous, unusual flight,
That for so long gave torment to the heavens,
Awakened suns and meteors and storms,
Imparted brilliance to the stars and lightning;
And amplitude: they had
Sufficient heat and shade for all the World,
Enough to incubate an "on beyond."

Un día, raramente
desmayada a la tierra,
yo me adormí en las felpas profundas de este bosque. . .
¡Soñé divinas cosas!
Una sonrisa tuya me despertó, paréceme. . .
¡Y no siento mis alas!. . .
¿Mis alas?. . .

Yo las vi deshacerse entre mis brazos. . .
¡Era como un deshielo!

NOCTURNO

Fuera, la noche en veste de tragedia solloza
como una enorme viuda pegada a mis cristales.

Mi cuarto. . .
Por un bello milagro de la luz y del fuego
mi cuarto es una gruta de oro y gemas raras;
tiene un musgo suave, tan hondo de tapices,
y es tan vívida y cálida, tan dulce, que me creo
dentro de un corazón.

¡Mi lecho que está en blanco es blanco y vaporoso
como flor de inocencia,
como espuma de vicio!
Esta noche hace insomnio;
hay noches negras, negras, que llevan en la frente
una rosa de sol. . .
en estas noches negras y claras no se duerme.

¡Y yo te amo, Invierno!
Yo te imagino viejo,
yo te imagino sabio,
con un divino cuerpo de mármol palpitante
que arrastra como un manto regio el peso del Tiempo. . .
Invierno, yo te amo y soy la Primavera. . .
yo sonroso, tú nievas;

One day when I lay strangely
Exhausted on the earth,
I fell asleep upon the forest's soft, deep plush.
I dreamed things most divine!
It seems to me a smile of yours awakened me.
I do not feel my wings!
My wings?

I saw them melt away between my arms.
It was just like a thaw!

NOCTURNE

Outside, the sad night clothed in tragedy's garments is sobbing,
Just like a huge widow who holds her face close to my window.

My room. . .
Through a beautiful miracle wrought by the fire and the light,
My room is a grotto of gold and of very rare gems;
It has a deep moss that is fashioned from tapestries' softness,
And it is so vivid, so warm and so sweet, I imagine
Myself in a heart.

My bed, all arrayed in pure white, is as white and as cloudlike
As the flower of innocence,
As the froth upon vice.
This night makes me sleepless;
Black nights come at times, oh so black, yet that wear on their brow
A bright rose like the sun.
Nobody can sleep on the nights that are black and yet bright.

I love you, O Winter!
I imagine you old,
I imagine you wise,
With body divinely created of quivering marble,
That trails like the mantles of royalty Time's heavy weight.
O Winter, I love you, and I am the Springtime.
I am rosy; you, snow;

tú, porque todo sabes,
yo, porque todo sueño. . .

. . .¡Amémonos por eso!. . .
Sobre mi lecho en blanco,
tan blanco y vaporoso como flor de inocencia,
como espuma de vicio,
Invierno, Invierno, Invierno,
¡caigamos en un ramo de rosas y lirios!

You, because you know all,
I, because I dream all.

Let us then love each other!
On my bed dressed in white,
As white and as cloudlike as innocence' fragile white flower,
As the froth upon vice,
Winter, Winter, O Winter,
Come now; let us fall in a cluster of roses and lilies!

ALFONSINA STORNI

CUADRADOS Y ANGULOS

Casas enfiladas, casas enfiladas,
Casas enfiladas.
Cuadrados, cuadrados, cuadrados.
Casas enfiladas
Las gentes ya tienen el alma cuadrada,
ideas en fila
y ángulo en la espalda.
Yo misma he vertido ayer una lágrima,
Dios mío, cuadrada.

HOMBRE PEQUENITO

Hombre pequeñito, hombre pequeñito,
suelta a tu canario que quiere volar. . .
yo soy el canario, hombre pequeñito,
déjame saltar.

Estuve en tu jaula, hombre pequeñito,
hombre pequeñito que jaula me das.
Digo pequeñito porque no me entiendes,
ni me entenderás.

Tampoco te entiendo, pero mientras tanto
ábreme la jaula, que quiero escapar;
hombre pequeñito, te amé media hora,
no me pidas más.

LA QUE COMPRENDE. . .

Con la cabeza negra caída hacia adelante
está la mujer bella, la de mediana edad,
postrada de rodillas, y un Cristo agonizante
desde su duro leño la mira con piedad.

ALFONSINA STORNI

SQUARES AND ANGLES

Houses in a row, houses in a row,
Houses in a row.
Block after block, block after block,
Houses in a row.
People even have rectangular-shaped souls,
Ideas in a line,
And angles on their backs.
Even I myself shed yesterday a tear,
That was . . . my goodness! . . . square.

DEAR LITTLE MAN

O my dear little man, O my dear little man,
Free your canary, as it wants to fly away;
For I am your canary, my dear little man;
O let me hop and play.

I went inside your cage, O my dear little man,
O little man, within whose cage I now am penned.
I call you "little," for you do not comprehend me,
Will never comprehend.

Nor am I comprehending you, but in the meantime
Please open that cage door, as I wish liberty;
O my dear little man, I loved you half an hour;
So ask no more from me.

THE ONE WHO UNDERSTANDS

The pretty woman, middle-aged, is down on bended knee,
With her black head bent forward in a reverential fashion,
And there a Christ who is enduring death's last agony
From His hard wooden cross above regards her with compassion.

En los ojos la carga de una enorme tristeza,
en el seno la carga del hijo por nacer,
al pie del blanco Cristo que está sangrando reza:
—¡Señor: el hijo mío que no nazca mujer!

PESO ANCESTRAL

Tú me dijiste: no lloró mi padre;
tú me dijiste: no lloró mi abuelo;
no han llorado los hombres de mi raza,
eran de acero.

Así diciendo te brotó una lágrima
y me cayó en la boca. . .; más veneno
yo no he bebido nunca en otro vaso
así pequeño.

Débil mujer, pobre mujer que entiende,
dolor de siglos conocí al beberlo.
Oh, el alma mía soportar no puede
todo su peso.

DOLOR

Quisiera esta tarde divina de octubre
pasear por la orilla lejana del mar;

que la arena de oro y las aguas verdes
y los cielos puros me vieran pasar. . .

Ser alta, soberbia, perfecta, quisiera,
como una romana, para concordar

con las grandes olas, y las rocas muertas
y las anchas playas que ciñen el mar.

Within her eyes weighs heavily enormous tribulation,
Within her body, heavily, unborn humanity.
She at the foot of that white bleeding Christ makes supplication,
"Lord, may my child not be a woman child, I beg of Thee."

ANCESTRAL WEIGHT

You said to me, "My father did not weep."
You said to me, "Grandfather did not cry.
The menfolk of my race have never wept.
They were of steel."

And as you spoke a tear gushed from your eye,
And then fell down upon my mouth; more poison
I never drank in any other glass
That was so small.

Weak, pitiable woman who can understand,
I knew the pain of centuries on drinking,
Alas, my soul can not endure the burden
Of all its weight.

PAIN

I should like on this divine October evening
To be walking far away beside the sea;

That on passing, golden sand and greenish waters
And the limpid sky above might look on me.

I should like to be tall, arrogant, and perfect,
Like a Roman woman, thus in harmony

With the mighty waves and lifeless rock formations
And the shores whose wide expanses gird the sea.

Con el paso lento y los ojos fríos
y la boca muda dejarme llevar;

ver cómo se rompen las olas azules
contra los granitos y no parpadear;

ver cómo las aves rapaces se comen
los peces pequeños y no suspirar;

pensar que pudieran las frágiles barcas
hundirse en las aguas y no despertar;

ver que se adelanta, la garganta libre,
el hombre más bello; no desear amar. . .

Perder la mirada, distraídamente,
perderla y que nunca la vuelva a encontrar;

y, figura erguida entre cielo y playa,
sentirme el olvido perenne del mar.

Let myself be borne along with measured footsteps,
With cold eyes, and mouth refusing word or cry;

See the waves of blue that break against the granite,
Yet not even show the blinking of an eye;

See the birds that are rapaciously devouring
Little fishes, yet not breathe a single sigh;

Think how fragile boats could sink within the waters,
Yet not feel alarm or be disturbed thereby.

See a handsome man advance with throat uncovered,
Yet not feel desire to love arise in me.

Lose my glance in absentminded contemplation,
Lose it so that it is lost eternally.

Feel myself, upon the shore beneath the heavens,
The perennial oblivion of the sea.

JUANA DE IBARBOUROU

VIDA-GARFIO

Amante, no me lleves, si muero, al camposanto.
A flor de tierra abre mi fosa, junto al riente
alboroto divino de alguna pajarera,
o junto a la encantada charla de alguna fuente.

A flor de tierra, amante. Casi sobre la tierra,
donde el sol me caliente los huesos, y mis ojos,
alargados en tallos, suban a ver de nuevo
la lámpara salvaje de los ocasos rojos.

A flor de tierra, amante. Que el tránsito así sea
más breve. Yo presiento
la lucha de mi carne por volver hacia arriba,
por sentir en sus átomos la frescura del viento.

Yo sé que acaso nunca allá abajo mis manos
podrán estarse quietas,
que siempre, como topos, arañarán la tierra
en medio de las sombras estrujadas y prietas.

Arrójame semillas. Yo quiero que se enraícen
en la greda amarilla de mis huesos menguados.
¡Por la parda escalera de las raíces vivas
yo subiré a mirarte en los lirios morados!

LA INQUIETUD FUGAZ

He mordido manzanas y he besado tus labios.
Me he abrazado a los pinos olorosos y negros.
Hundí, inquieta, mis manos en el agua que corre.
He huroneado en la selva milenaria de cedros

JUANA DE IBARBOUROU

CLINGING TO LIFE

If I should die, beloved, take me to no cemetery,
But let my sepulcher be opened just below the ground,
Close to some aviary with its heavenly laughing noise,
Or else close to a fountain with its charming chatting sound.

Beloved, just below the ground. And almost on the earth,
So that the sun may give my bones its warmth, and where my eyes,
Prolonged within the stems of plants may rise to see anew
The sunsets light their savage lamp in crimson western skies.

Beloved, just below the ground. Let the transition thus
Be briefer. I foretell
My body will be struggling always to return above,
So it may feel the freshness of the wind in every cell.

I am quite certain that my hands when underground can never
Stay quietly at rest;
But as if moles, they will be always scratching at the earth,
Within the darkness where they are so crowded and compressed.

Throw seeds upon me. I desire that they might there take root
Within the yellow clay remaining from my wretched bones.
Along the dark gray ladder that the living roots have made
I shall ascend to look at you from lilies' purple tones.

FLEETING RESTLESSNESS

I have bitten into apples; I have kissed your lips.
I have embraced dark pine trees with their fragrant scent.
Unquiet, I submerged my hands in running water.
I have hunted in the thousand-year old cedar wood

que cruza la pradera como una sierpe grave,
y he corrido por todos los pedrosos caminos
que ciñen como fajas la ventruda montaña.

¡Oh amado, no te irrites por mi inquietud sin tregua!
¡Oh amado, no me riñas porque cante y me ría!
Ha de llegar un día en que he de estarme quieta,
¡ay, por siempre, por siempre!,
con las manos cruzadas y apagados los ojos,
con los oídos sordos y con la boca muda,
y los pies andariegos en reposo perpetuo
sobre la tierra negra.
Y estará roto el vaso de cristal de mi risa
en la grieta obstinada de mis labios cerrados.

Entonces, aunque digas:—¡Anda!, ya no andaré.
Y aunque me digas:—¡Canta!, no volveré a cantar.
Me iré desmenuzando en quietud y en silencio
bajo la tierra negra,
mientras encima mío se oirá zumbar la vida
como una abeja ebria.

¡Oh, déjame que guste el dulzor del momento
fugitivo e inquieto!

¡Oh, deja que la rosa desnuda de mi boca
se te oprima a los labios!

Después será cenizas bajo la tierra negra.

That winds across the prairie like a solemn serpent,
And I have journeyed over all the stony roads
That gird the paunchy mountain as if they were its sashes.

Beloved, let my restlessness not anger you!
Beloved, do not chide my singing and my laughing!
A day will come on which I shall remain quite silent,
Alas, for evermore!
With folded hands and with my eyes devoid of light,
With ears unhearing and my mouth entirely mute,
And with my wandering feet in permanent repose
Below the blackish earth.
The crystal vessel of my laughter will be broken
Within the crevice firmly held by my closed lips.

Although you may say "Go!" I shall no longer go.
Although you may sing "Sing!" I shall not sing again.
I shall be slowly crumbling in the quietude
Below the blackish earth,
While up above me life will still be heard to buzz
As if a drunken bee.

Oh let me taste the sweetness of the present moment,
So fleeting and unquiet!

Oh let the naked rosebud of my mouth be pressed
Against your own lips now!

Soon it will be but ashes under blackish earth.

DESPECHO

¡Ah, que estoy cansada! Me he reído tanto,
tanto, que a mis ojos ha asomado el llanto;
tanto, que este rictus que contrae mi boca
es un rastro extraño de mi risa loca.

Tanto, que esta intensa palidez que tengo
(como en los retratos de viejo abolengo),
es por la fatiga de la loca risa
que en todos mis nervios su sopor desliza.

¡Ah, que estoy cansada! Déjame que duerma,
pues, como la angustia, la alegría enferma.
¡Qué rara ocurrencia decir que estoy triste!
¿Cuándo más alegre que ahora, me viste?

¡Mentira! No tengo ni dudas, ni celos,
ni inquietud, ni angustias, ni penas, ni anhelos.
Si brilla en mis ojos la humedad del llanto,
es por el esfuerzo de reírme tanto. . .

MUJER

Si yo fuera hombre, ¡qué hartazgo de luna,
de sombra y silencio me había de dar!
¡Cómo, noche a noche, solo ambularía
por los campos quietos y por frente al mar!

Si yo fuera hombre, ¡qué extraño, qué loco,
tenaz vagabundo que había de ser!
¡Amigo de todos los largos caminos
que invitan a ir lejos para no volver!

Cuando así me acosan ansias andariegas,
¡qué pena tan honda me da ser mujer!

DEJECTION

Oh how weary I am! I have laughed for so long,
For so long that the tears now appear in my eyes;
For so long that the twitch now contracting my mouth
Is the trace my mad laughter has left in this guise.

For so long, this intense look of pallor I wear,
(That the portraits of all my old ancestors show,)
Merely comes from fatigue caused by laughing so madly,
And the lethargy that all my nerves sadly know.

Oh how weary I am! Let me now fall to sleep,
For if anguish brings illness, it comes from joy too.
How peculiar it is that you think I am sad!
When, if ever, have I appeared gayer to you?

What a lie! I feel naught of unrest or of longing;
Nor do feelings of pain, doubt or jealousy throng.
If there shines in my eyes the faint moisture of weeping,
It is due to the effort of laughing so long.

WOMAN

Oh, if I were a man, how I should get my fill
Of silence and of shade, and of the moon's fair light!
How I should wander then while facing toward the sea,
And through the quiet fields, alone night after night!

Oh, if I were a man, then what a strange, erratic,
Persistent vagabond I should become no doubt!
A friend of all the roads whose lengthiness invites
Each one to travel far and never turn about!

When thus desires to roam beset me urgently,
How deeply I regret my femininity!

ENRIQUE BANCHS

BALBUCEO

Triste está la casa nuestra,
triste, desde que te has ido.
Todavía queda un poco
de tu calor en el nido.

Yo también estoy un poco
triste desde que te has ido;
pero sé que alguna tarde
llegarás de nuevo al nido.

¡Si supieras cuánto, cuánto
la casa y yo te queremos!
Algún día cuando vuelvas
verás cuánto te queremos.

Nunca podría decirte
todo lo que te queremos:
es como un montón de estrellas
todo lo que te queremos.

Si tú no volvieras nunca,
más vale que yo me muera. . .;
pero siento que no quieres,
no quieres que yo me muera.

Bien querida que te fuiste,
¿no es cierto que volverás?
para que no estemos tristes,
¿no es cierto que volverás?

ENRIQUE BANCHS

STAMMERING

Our house is sad, is sad
Since you have gone away.
Some of your warmth remains
Within the nest today.

I too am somewhat sad
Since you have gone away;
I know though you will come
Back to the nest some day.

If you knew how, how much,
The house and I love you!
Some day when you return,
You will see how we love you.

I never could express
How greatly we love you;
It seems a heap of stars,
So greatly we love you.

If you should not return,
It is best that I should die.
I feel you do not wish,
Not wish that I should die.

Dear love that went away,
Will you not surely come?
So we may not be sad,
Will you not surely come?

CANCIONCILLA

No quería amarte,
ramo de azahar;
no debía amarte;
te tengo que amar.

Tan manso vivía . . . ,
rosa de rosal,
tan quieto vivía:
me has herido mal.

¿No éramos amigos?
Vara de alelí,
si éramos amigos,
¿por qué herirme así?

Cuidé no te amara,
paloma torcaz.
¿Quién que no te amara?
Ya no puedo más.

Tanto sufrimiento,
zorzal de jardín,
duro sufrimiento
me ha doblado al fin.

Suspiros, sollozos,
pájaro del mar;
sollozos, suspiros,
me quieren matar.

A LITTLE SONG

I did not want to love you,
O orange-blossom bough;
I ought not to have loved you;
I have to love you now.

So tranquilly I lived,
O rose so fair to see,
So quietly I lived;
You badly wounded me.

Were we not once good friends,
O gillyflower spray?
If we were once good friends,
Why wound me in this way?

I took care not to love you,
O my dear turtle-dove.
Whoever would not love you?
I am worn out with love.

So much of suffering,
O garden thrush so sweet,
My grievous suffering
At last brought me defeat.

My sighs and bitter sobs,
O bird that loves the sea,
My bitter sobs and sighs
Will end by killing me.

EL VOTO

¿Cuál conjunción de estrellas me ha tornado coplero?. . .
Mi planta para el carro de Harmonía es muy breve,
y ante tu templo, ¡oh Musa!, yo soy como un romero
que al ara, toda lumbre y lino y plata y nieve,
lleno de miedos santos a llegar no se atreve. . .

Lejano es ese día. Fuí a la carpintería,
y turbando el chirrido de las sierras, entonce
clamé al roble, al escoplo y a la cerrajería,
al cepillo que canta y a la tuerca de bronce,
a las ensambladuras y al hueco para el gonce.

Y dije: olor de pino, sabor de selva y río,
rizo de la viruta, nitidez del formón,
tornillo, gusanito tenaz lleno de brío,
glóbulo saltarín del nivel, precisión
de escuadra, de compás, de plomo en suspensión.

Bienvenida a este nuevo trabajador de robles,
porque él hará hemistiquios, ya sobre el pino esprús,
ya en el nogal, que es digno de cuajar gestos nobles,
o el sándalo oloroso o el ébano, que en luz
brilla por negro y brilla porque él hace la cruz.

Bienvenida a este nuevo trabajador del pino,
que moverá el martillo cual rima de canción,
al hacer la mortaja, la cuna o el divino
talle de los violines o el recio mascarón
que habla con los delfines desde la embarcación;

la puerta que se abre cuando un amigo llega;
la mesa en que partimos el pan con los hermanos,
y el ropero, el ropero familiar que doblega
los anchos anaqueles bajo rimeros vanos
de lienzos que de tanto blancor están lozanos. . .

¿Cuál conjunción de estrellas me ha tornado coplero?

THE VOW

What conjunction of stars made me be a poor poet?
My short foot is ill suited to Harmony's chariot;
And, O Muse, in thy temple I am as a pilgrim
Who through reverent fear does not dare to draw nigh
To the altar,—all light, silver, linen, and snow.

Far away is the day that I went to the shop
Of the carpenter, where while disturbing the screech
Of the saws, I laid claim to the oak-wood and chisel;
Locksmith's forge; singing plane; shining lock-nut of bronze;
And the mortises made for the tenons and hinges.

And I said, "Pine's fresh fragrance and savor of woods
And of river; curled shavings; and brightness of firmer;
Screw and auger, tenacious and showing great spirit;
Dancing bubble of level; and utmost precision
Of the square, and the compass, and lead in the plumb-line.

"Welcome now this new worker in oak-wood, for he
Will make hemistichs, now on the spruce; now on walnut
That is worthy of noble adornment; or sandalwood
Sweetly scented; or ebony gleaming when light shines,
Due to blackness and pride in its use for the crucifix.

"Welcome now this new worker in pine-wood, for he
Will be swinging the hammer like rhythm of a song,
As he fashions the casket; the cradle; the body
Of a fine violin; the stout figurehead, soon
To converse with the dolphins from up on the ship;

"The wide door that is opened when friends are arriving;
The long table on which we break bread with our brothers;
And the clothespress, the family clothespress that bends
Its broad shelves under large heavy piles of prized linen,
That seems quite luxurious, due to its whiteness."

What conjunction of stars made me be a poor poet?

TORNASOLANDO EL FLANCO

Tornasolando el flanco a su sinuoso
paso va el tigre suave como un verso
y la ferocidad pule cual terso
topacio al ojo seco y vigoroso.

Y desperezа el músculo alevoso
de los ijares, lánguido y perverso
y se recuesta lento en el disperso
otoño de las hojas. El reposo. . .

El reposo en la selva silenciosa.
La testa chata entre las garras finas
y el ojo fijo, impávido custodio.

Espía mientras bate con nerviosa
cola el haz de las férulas vecinas,
en reprimido acecho. . .así es mi odio.

THE TIGER

His flank like watered silk, the tiger goes
With sinuous step as smooth as poetry,
And in his strong cold eye, ferocity
Shines brightly as a burnished topaz glows.

On stretching then, the treacherous muscle shows
Within his side; with slow diablerie
He goes to make his bed quite languidly
On scattered autumn of the leaves. Repose. . .

Repose within the woods where silence reigns.
Flat head between fine paws and fixed his eyes,
Calm guards against all dangers that await.

While nervous tail a constant beat maintains
Upon the fennel that is near, he spies,
His ambush held in check. . .so is my hate.

RAFAEL ALBERTO ARRIETA

LA VOZ AUSENTE

¡Ah, mi lejano país!
Cielo azul, río de nácar,
tierra en que dejé mi esfuerzo
y, con el esfuerzo, mi alma!

(¡Feliz tú que la verás!)

¡Ah, los árboles amigos!
¡Sombra y música! ¡Alabada
sombra que supo envolverme!
¡Cancioncilla de las ramas!

(¡Feliz tú que la verás!)

¡Ah, mi hogar, nido deshecho
del que ya no queda nada!
Dícenme que sus cimientos
sirvieron para otra casa. . .

(¡Feliz tú que la verás!)

¡Ah, rinconcito del valle
donde mis padres descansan!
La cruz de palo, me dicen,
ya fué convertida en llamas. . .

(¡Feliz tú que la verás!)

¡Ah, mi amor, mi dulce amor,
la que mi regreso aguarda!
Dícenme que el sufrimiento
su cabeza blanqueó en canas. . .

Feliz tú que la verás,
romero, ¡y tú no la amas!
Feliz tú que la verás. . .
¡y no es a ti a quien aguarda!

RAFAEL ALBERTO ARRIETA

THE ABSENT VOICE

Ah, my distant fatherland!
With sky of blue and pearly river;
The land in which I left my courage,
And with my courage, left my soul!

(O happy you, for you will see her!)

Ah, the trees that were so friendly!
Sweet shade and music! How I praise
The shade that would envelop me!
The little song made by the branches!

(O happy you, for you will see her!)

Ah, my home, a nest destroyed,
Of which no longer aught remains!
I have been told that its foundation
Did duty for another house. .

(O happy you, for you will see her!)

Ah, small corner of the valley
In which my parents lie at rest!
I have been told the cross of wood
Was once converted into flames.

(O happy you, for you will see her!)

Ah, my love, my own sweet love,
Who is awaiting my return!
I have been told that suffering
Has caused her hair to turn to white.

Happy you, for you will see her,
O pilgrim, and you do not love her!
O happy you, for you will see her.
And you are not the one awaited!

EN UN CEMENTERIO ABANDONADO

El paso sigiloso, la voz queda,
votiva el alma, entre las tumbas. . . Yacen
aquí, bajo estas lápidas, humildes
serranos del lugar. Nada revelan
las pobres inscripciones, pero todo,
entre dos fechas simples, lo adivinan
tu corazón y el mío. Mis anhelos,
tus sueños, nuestro amor, tienen raíces
intrincadas e ignotas aquí abajo,
en la comunidad indestructible
del humano dolor. También alguno
de los aquí dormidos, miró un día,
en otra tarde como ésta, el cielo,
la línea de las cumbres, esos álamos,
el sol en el camino, el verde valle,
y oyó cantar al Rey-del-bosque. . . Brillo
de juventud y de serena dicha,
como en tus ojos, en los suyos hubo,
y fué su paz hermana de la nuestra,
y esta alegría de vivir que tengo
¡túvola él ante el paisaje mismo!

Cementerio olvidado, ya no viene
a renovar tus flores el Recuerdo;
sólo la noche deja en ti sus lágrimas
y el viento su sollozo. La ruinosa
pirca, y el laberinto de malezas,
y las tronchadas cruces, son la muerte
sobre la muerte. . . Mas la vida triunfa
y con ardiente ímpetu avasalla
en pujante irrupción. Inciensa el aire
la oculta piperina; abeja acróbata
acaba de posarse en fino tallo
y hamácase feliz, tornasolada
al chispeante vaivén; cantan los élitros
entre el zarzal; trasvuela y centellea
libélula joyante; las retamas,
sus llamitas inmóviles encienden

IN AN ABANDONED CEMETERY

With silent step and with a lowered voice
And votive soul among the sepulchers. . .
Here there are lying underneath these stones
Some humble mountain people of the place.
Naught is revealed by all these poor inscriptions,
But everything, between two simple dates,
Your heart and mine can guess. My deepest longings,
Your dreams, and our own mutual love have roots,
Unknown and intricate, down under here,
In indestructible community
Of human suffering. And some one too
Of those now sleeping here observed one day,
Another evening just like this, the sky,
The line formed by the peaks, the poplar trees,
The sun upon the road, and the green valley;
He heard the singing of the "forest-king."
There was the glow of tranquil happiness
And youth within his eyes like that in yours,
And his own peace was sister of our peace,
And this same joy in living that I have,
He had it, seeing the same scenery!

Forgotten cemetery, now Remembrance
No longer comes here to renew your flowers;
The night alone now leaves its tears in you,
And just the wind, its sobs. The ruined wall
Of stone and labyrinth of underbrush,
And mutilated crosses are themselves
Death over death. . .But life is triumphing
And with its ardent impetus prevails
In powerful irruption. In the air
Is incense from the hidden piperine;
The acrobatic bee has just alighted
Upon a slender stem and gaily swings,
Made iridescent by the sparkling sway;
Elytra sing midst brambles; and there flies
And gleams the very glossy dragon-fly.
The furze is lighting its small steady flames

sobre las tumbas; la ebriedad de un pájaro
invisible, desgrana en los cristales
del éter, su maravilloso trino;
y al lado mío, por el brazo único
de mutilada cruz, va tambaleante,
una hormiguita con su blanco pétalo
como una vela sola por el mar. . .

¡Oh, mujer mía! Aquí besarte quiero,
entre las tumbas que la sierra acoge
como en regazo maternal y baña,
con su tibieza, el sol. ¡Dame tu boca!
Bajo tus pies, la tierra estremecida
tendrá un latido de ternura humana,
y el corazón de polvo que la nutre
florecerá, tal vez, en una estrella
roja, sobre el vestigio de tu planta.

Above the tombs; and the intoxication
Of a bird not visible is scattering
In the crystals of the ether wondrous trills;
And at my side, along the only arm
Of the mutilated cross goes staggering
A tiny ant transporting her white petal
Just like a single sail upon the sea.

Oh my dear wife! I wish to kiss you here
Among the sepulchers the mountain shelters
As in a mother's lap and that the sun
Is bathing with its warmth. Give me your mouth!
Beneath your feet, the earth then made to tremble
Will have a throb of human tenderness,
And the heart of dust that gives it nourishment
Perhaps will blossom in a crimson star
Above the footprint that your foot has made.

RAFAEL AREVALO MARTINEZ

LOS HOMBRES-LOBOS

Primero dije "hermanos" y les tendí las manos;
después en mis corderos hicieron mal sus robos;
y entonces en mi alma murió la voz de hermanos
y me acerqué a mirarlos: ¡y todos eran lobos!

¿Qué sucedía en mi alma que así marchaba a ciegas,
en mi alma pobre y triste que sueña y se encariña?
¿Cómo no vi en sus trancos las bestias andariegas?
¿Cómo no vi en sus ojos instintos de rapiña?

Después yo, también lobo, dejé el sendero sano;
después yo, también lobo, caí no sé en qué lodos;
y entonces en cada uno de ellos tuve un hermano
y me acerqué a mirarlos: ¡y eran hombres todos!

COMO LOS CIPRESES. . .

Poeta, dijeron, ¿por qué prodigaste
tus rubias estrofas, como un áureo engaste
dado a los diamantes de tu vida triste,
para muchas almas idas que lloraste,
para muchos cuerpos blancos que quisiste?

¿Y por qué callaste como un muerto cuando
se murió tu madre; y tu alma armoniosa
no ha tenido un canto ni para tu esposa
ni para tu hijo?
—Porque la angustiosa
copa de la vida se bebe callando.

Los grandes dolores son mudos, señores.
Si nuestras tristezas contamos a veces
cuando nos enlutan los grandes dolores,
cuando nos conmueven las grandes ternuras,
nos quedamos mudos, como los cipreses,
como los cipreses de la sepulturas.

RAFAEL AREVALO MARTINEZ

THE MEN-WOLVES

At first I called them "brothers," with my hands extended;
But soon their thieving in my sheepfold was begun;
The call of brotherhood then in my soul was ended;
Approaching them, I saw that they were wolves, each one!

What happened in my soul that it was so unseeing,
In my poor soul that is so prone to love and dream?
I should have seen in their long strides the roving being,
And in their eyes the cruel predatory gleam.

Since then I also left the straight road for another;
A wolf myself, in what deep mud holes I would fall!
Then I could recognize in each of them a brother;
Approaching them, I saw that they were men; yes, all!

LIKE THE CYPRESSES

They said, "O poet, why did you spend lavishly
Your ruddy stanzas, like a setting of pure gold,
Around the diamonds of your sad, gloomy life,
For numberless departed souls for whom you wept,
For numberless white bodies that you one time loved?

"And why did you remain as silent as a corpse
The time your mother died? Why is it that your soul
So full of music has no poems for your wife
Or for your son?"
"Because the goblet of one's life
Filled to the brim with anguish must be drunk in silence.

"The greatest griefs and pains are ever silent, sirs.
If it is true we tell our sadnesses at times,
Whenever great affliction covers us with mourning,
And when our hearts are moved with greatest tenderness,
Then we remain quite silent like the cypresses,
Just like the cypresses above the sepulchers."

RAMON LOPEZ VELARDE

EL RETORNO MALEFICO

Mejor será no regresar al pueblo,
al edén subvertido que se calla
en la mutilación de la metralla.

Hasta los fresnos mancos,
los dignatarios de cúpula oronda,
han de rodar las quejas de la torre
acribillada en los vientos de fronda.

Y la fusilería grabó en la cal
de todas las paredes
de la aldea espectral,
negros y aciagos mapas,
porque en ellos leyese el hijo pródigo
al volver a su umbral
en un anochecer de maleficio,
a la luz de petróleo de una mecha,
su esperanza deshecha.

Cuando la tosca llave enmohecida
tuerza la chirriante cerradura,
en la añeja clausura
del zaguán, los dos púdicos
medallones de yeso,
entornando los párpados narcóticos,
se mirarán y se dirán: "¿Qué es eso?"

Y yo entraré con pies advenedizos
hasta el patio agorero
en que hay un brocal ensimismado,
con un cubo de cuero
goteando su gota categórica
como un estribillo plañidero.

Si el sol inexorable, alegre y tónico,
hace hervir a las fuentes catecúmenas
en que bañábase mi sueño crónico;
si se afana la hormiga;

RAMON LOPEZ VELARDE

THE MALEFICENT RETURN

It is not wise to go back to the town,
To paradise in ruins, now all silent,
Amidst the mutilation made by grapeshot.

The crippled ash trees even,
The dignitaries with their pompous domes,
When winds are blowing must surround with foliage
The sad laments of that shot-ridden tower.

And fusileers engraved upon the lime
Of each one of the walls
Within the spectral village,
Some black and gloomy maps,
So that the son who as a prodigal
Returned to his own threshold
When night was falling midst an evil spell,
Might read on them by light an oil wick casts
His hopes now all destroyed.

When the crude key on which the rust has gathered
Turns in the lock that makes a creaking noise,
Within the old enclosure
The entry forms, two modest
Medallions made of plaster,
Half opening drugged eyelids will inquire,
While looking at each other, "What is that?"

And I shall enter with a stranger's steps
The foreboding patio
In which there stands an absent-minded well-curb
With bucket made of leather,
That categorically drips its drop
That seems a sad refrain of mournful weeping.

If the relentless, cheerful, tonic sun
Should make the sophomoric fountains boil
In which my chronic sleep might then be bathing;
And should the ant be busy;

si en los techos resuena y se fatiga
de los buches de tórtola el reclamo
que entre las telarañas zumba y zumba;
mi sed de amar será como una argolla
empotrada en la losa de una tumba.

Las golondrinas nuevas, renovando
con sus noveles picos alfareros
los nidos tempraneros;
bajo el ópalo insigne
de los atardeceres monacales,
el lloro de recientes recentales
por la ubérrima ubre prohibida
de la vaca, rumiante y faraónica,
que al párvulo intimida;
campanario de timbre novedoso;
remozados altares;
el amor amoroso
de las parejas pares;
noviazgos de muchachas
frescas y humildes, como humildes coles,
y que la mano dan por el postigo
a la luz de dramáticos faroles;
alguna señorita
que canta en algún piano
alguna vieja aria;
el gendarme que pita. . .
. . .Y una íntima tristeza reaccionaria.

If on the roofs there should resound till wearied,
Enticement from the bills of turtle-doves,
Which hums and hums amongst the spider webs;
My thirst for loving would be like a ring
Embedded in the slab above a tomb.

The swallows, new arrivals, now renewing
The early nests with beaks that still are new
At working with the clay;
Below the opal tint
Peculiar to monastic eventides,
The crying of the new-born baby calves
For banished overflowing udders
Of ruminating Pharaonic cows,
Which frighten the small child;
The belfry with its fluctuating tones;
Rejuvenated altars;
The love so full of love
Of married pairs in pairs;
The fiancés of maidens
Extending their hands out between the shutters,
As fresh and humble as the humble cabbage,
By that light cast there by dramatic street lamps;
Some young unmarried lady
Who sings at some piano
Some ancient aria;
The gendarme with his whistle. . .
. . .And inwardly reactionary sadness.

JORGE LUIS BORGES

LA GUITARRA

He mirado la Pampa
de un patiecito de la calle Sarandí en Buenos Aires.
Cuando entré no la vi.
Estaba acurrucada
en lo profundo de una brusca guitarra.
Sólo se desmelenó
al entreverar la diestra las cuerdas.
No sé lo que azuzaban;
a lo mejor fué un triste del Norte
pero yo vi la Pampa.
Vi muchas brazadas de cielo
sobre un manojito de pasto.
Vi una loma que arrinconan
quietas distancias
mientras leguas y leguas
caen desde lo alto.
Vi el campo donde cabe
Dios sin haber de inclinarse,
vi el único lugar de la tierra
donde puede caminar Dios a sus anchas.
Vi la Pampa cansada
que antes horrorizaron los malones
y hoy apaciguan en quietud maciza las parvas.
De un tirón vi todo eso
mientras se desesperaban las cuerdas
en un compás tan zarandeado como éste.
(La vi también a ella
cuyo recuerdo aguarda en toda música.)
Hasta que en brusco cataclismo
se allanó la guitarra encabritada
y estrújome el silencio
y hurañamente volvió el vivir a estancarse.

JORGE LUIS BORGES

THE GUITAR

I looked upon the Pampa
While standing in a little patio in Buenos Aires.
At first I did not see it,
For it was folded tightly
Deep in the confines of a rude guitar.
It was unsettled only
When the strings were intermingled by a hand.
I do not know its message.
At best it was a gloomy Northern song,
But I could see the Pampa.
I saw the fathoms of the sky
Above a bit of pastureland.
I saw a little hill forsaken
By quiet distances,
And meanwhile leagues and leagues
Are falling from the height.
I saw the field where God
Has room without the need of bending over;
I saw the only place on earth
Where God can travel wholly at His ease.
I saw the weary Pampa
Once horrified by sudden raids,
And now reposing in the steady calm of heaps of corn.
At once I saw all that
Just as the strings were voicing their despair
By means of measures quite as varied as the ones found here.
(Moreover I saw her
Whose memory awaits me in all music.)
Then in a sudden cataclysm
The rampant old guitar became subdued
And silence bruised me,
And diffidently, living then returned to its stagnation.

UN PATIO

Con la tarde
se cansaron los dos o tres colores del patio.
La gran franqueza de la luna llena
ya no entusiasma su habitual firmamento.
Hoy que está crespo el cielo
dirá la agorería que ha muerto un angelito.
Patio, cielo encauzado.
El patio es la ventana
por donde Dios mira las almas.
El patio es el declive
por el cual se derrama el cielo en la casa.
Serena
la eternidad espera en la encrucijada de estrellas.
Lindo es vivir en la amistad oscura
de un zaguán, de un alero y de un aljibe.

A PATIO

With evening
The two or three bright colors of the patio grow weary.
The openheartedness the full moon shows
No longer is enrapturing its wonted firmament.
Today when skies are angry,
The soothsayer believes a little angel must have died.
The patio, a channeled heaven.
The patio, a window
Through which God looks at souls.
The patio, the slope
Along which heaven spills within the house.
Serenely,
Eternity is waiting at the crossroad of the stars.
It is good to live within the humble favor
Of the vestibule, of eaves, and of a cistern.

JAIME TORRES BODET

ECO

¿Cómo pude arrancar,
con qué mano sin alma al árbol seco
en que la vida endureció sus savias
los tímidos renuevos de lo eterno?

Cambié
por un collar de frágiles palabras
un ánfora colmada de silencio.

¡Ay! ¿Por qué te maté dentro de mí,
Eternidad? Llevé tu cauce lento
a despeñarse en una
catarata de músicas vulgares
para mover las fábricas del eco. . .

Te dividí en minutos.
Rompí la adusta integridad del tiempo,
en cuyo ancho caudal, solemne, bogas.
Tuve miedo de ti, como de un vuelo.

Nada quedó después.
He roto, Vida, tu árbol más perfecto
para tejer guirnaldas con las hojas
y coger, en sus redes, los pájaros del viento.

Ahora miro el hueco que dejó
tu raíz en el suelo.

¡Y cada fibra rota
resucita sensible, dolorosa,
en las fibras desnudas de mis nervios!

JAIME TORRES BODET

ECHO

How could I tear away
With such a ruthless hand from the dry tree
Whose many years had caused its sap to harden,
Eternity's own timorous young sprouts?

I bartered
For a necklace formed of fragile words
An amphora filled brimmingly with silence.

Alas! Why did I kill you in my soul,
Eternity? I caused your sluggish flow
To hurl itself head-foremost
Within a cataract of vulgar music,
Thus to awaken echo's fabrications.

I split you into minutes.
I broke the grave integrity of time,
In whose wide stream you row in solemnness.
I was afraid of you, as of a flight.

Then there was nothing left.
Life, I have broken your most perfect tree,
So that I might weave garlands of the leaves
And catch within their snares the wind's small birds.

Now I perceive quite well the cavity
Your root left in the ground.

And each of the torn fibers
Resuscitates now sensitive and painful
Within the naked fibers of my nerves!

MUSICA

Amanecía tu voz
tan perezosa, tan blanda,
como si el día anterior
hubiera
llovido sobre tu alma. . .

Era, primero, un temblor
confuso del corazón,
una duda de poner
sobre los hielos del agua
el pie
desnudo de la palabra.

Después,
iba quedando la flor
de la emoción, enredada
a los hilos de tu voz
con esos garfios de escarcha
que el sol
desfleca en cintillos de agua.

Y se apagaba y se iba
poniendo blanca,
hasta dejar traslucir,
como la luna del alba
la luz
tierna de la madrugada.

Y se apagaba y se iba,
¡ay!, haciendo tan delgada
como la espuma de plata
de la playa,
como la espuma de plata
que deja ver, en la arena,
la forma de una pisada.

MUSIC

Your voice appeared at dawn
As lazy and as soft,
As if the day before
It had
Been raining on your soul.

It was a timorous trembling
Within the heart at first,
A doubt if you should set
Down on the water's ice
Your foot
Of language, all unshod.

And later,
There still remained the flower
Of your emotion, caught
Within your voice's fibers
With those large hooks of frost-work
That the sun
Flakes off in fluid ribbons.

And it was growing softer,
Becoming white,
Until one saw through it
Just like the moon at dawn
The soft
Pale light of early morning.

And it was growing softer,
Alas! becoming light
As silver-colored foam
Upon the seashore.
As silver-colored foam
Through which is seen the print
A foot made on the sand.

PABLO NERUDA

PUENTES

Puentes—arcos de acero azul adonde vienen
a dar su despedida los que pasan,—
por arriba los trenes,
por abajo las aguas,
enfermos de seguir un largo viaje
que principia, que sigue y nunca acaba.

Cielos—arriba—cielos,
y pájaros que pasan
sin detenerse, caminando como
los trenes y las aguas.
¿Qué maldición cayó sobre vosotros?
¿Qué esperáis en la noche densa y larga
con los brazos abiertos como un niño
que muere a la llegada de su hermana?

¿Qué voz de maldición pasiva y negra
sobre vosotros extendió sus alas,
para hacer que siguieran
el viaje que no acaba
los paisajes, la vida, el sol, la tierra,
los trenes y las aguas,
mientras la angustia inmóvil del acero
se hunde más en la tierra y más la clava?

PABLO NERUDA

BRIDGES

O bridges,—arches of blue steel to which these come
To say farewell as they are passing by,—
The trains that are above,
The waters down below,
Infirm from travelling so long a journey
That starts, continues, and is never ended.

The skies—above—the skies,
And birds that pass along
And never stop, while travelling as do
The waters and the trains.
What malediction fell upon your head?
For what do you wait there through long, dense nights,
With your two arms outstretched just like a child
Who dies on the arrival of his sister?

What voice of malediction, black and passive,
Has spread its wings out wide and covered you,
To make all things continue:
The journey with no end,
The landscapes, life itself, the sun, the earth,
The waters, and the trains,—
While the immobile anguish of the steel
Sinks further in the earth and pierces more?

WALKING AROUND

Sucede que me canso de ser hombre.
Sucede que entro en las sastrerías y en los cines
marchito, impenetrable, como un cisne de fieltro
navegando en un agua de origen y ceniza.

El olor de las peluquerías me hace llorar a gritos.
Sólo quiero un descanso de piedras o de lana,
sólo quiero no ver establecimientos ni jardines,
ni mercaderías, ni anteojos, ni ascensores.

Sucede que me canso de mis pies y mis uñas
y mi pelo y mi sombra.
Sucede que me canso de ser hombre.

Sin embargo sería delicioso
asustar a un notario con un lirio cortado
o dar muerte a una monja con un golpe de oreja.
Sería bello
ir por las calles con un cuchillo verde
y dando gritos hasta morir de frío.

No quiero seguir siendo raíz en las tinieblas,
vacilante, extendido, tiritando de sueño,
hacia abajo, en las tripas mojadas de la tierra,
absorbiendo y pensando, comiendo cada día.

No quiero para mí tantas desgracias.
No quiero continuar de raíz y de tumba,
de subterráneo solo, de bodega con muertos,
aterido, muriéndome de pena.

Por eso el día lunes arde como el petróleo
cuando me ve llegar con mi cara de cárcel,
y aulla en su transcurso como una rueda herida,
y da pasos de sangre caliente hacia la noche.

Y me empuja a ciertos rincones, a ciertas casas húmedas,
a hospitales donde los huesos salen por la ventana,

WALKING AROUND

It happens I am tired of being a man.
It happens that I enter tailor shops and movies
Impenetrable, withered, like a swan of felt
That navigates a water full of origins and ashes.

The odor of the barber shops makes me weep aloud.
I merely wish to find repose in stones or wool.
I merely wish to see no more establishments or gardens,
Or merchandise, or elevators, or eyeglasses.

It happens I am tired of my own feet and nails
And my own hair and shadow.
It happens I am tired of being a man.

It would, however, be delightful
To frighten a notary with a cut lily
Or give death to a nun with a blow upon her ear.
It would be lovely
To go along the streets with a green knife
While giving shouts until one dies of cold.

I do not want to go on as a root in total darkness,
Vacillating, spread out, shivering with sleep,
Downward, in the earth's wet bowels,
Thinking and absorbing, eating every day.

I do not want so many cares upon my head.
I do not want to go on being root and tomb,
A lonely cellar, a vault with dead men,
Benumbed with cold and perishing with pain.

That is the reason Monday burns as if it were petroleum
When it sees me arriving with my prisoner's face,
And howls along its course like a wounded wheel,
And takes its steps of hot blood toward the night.

And drives me into certain corners, to some damp houses,
To hospitals where bones go out through windows,

a ciertas zapaterías con olor a vinagre,
a calles espantosas como grietas.

Hay pájaros de color de azufre y horribles intestinos
colgando de las puertas de las casas que odio,
hay dentaduras olvidadas en una cafetera,
hay espejos
que debieran haber llorado de vergüenza y espanto,
hay paraguas en todas partes, y venenos y ombligos.

Yo paseo con calma, con ojos, con zapatos,
con furia, con olvido,
paso, cruzo oficinas y tiendas de ortopedia,
y patios donde hay ropas colgadas de un alambre:
calzoncillos, toallas y camisas que lloran
lentas lágrimas sucias.

To certain shoe stores with the smell of vinegar,
To streets as terrible as cracks.

There are sulphur-colored birds and horrible intestines
Hanging from the doors of houses I abhor;
There are dentures left forgotten in a coffeepot;
There are mirrors
That must have wept from shamc and fright;
There are umbrellas everywhere, and poisons and navels.

I walk around with calm, with eyes, with shoes,
With fury, with forgetfulness;
I go on, I pass through offices and orthopedic shops
And patios where clothes are hanging from a wire:
Some drawers, towels, and shirts that weep
Slow dirty tears.

BARCAROLA

Si solamente me tocaras el corazón,
si solamente pusieras tu boca en mi corazón,
tu fina boca, tus dientes,
si pusieras tu lengua como una flecha roja
allí donde mi corazón polvoriento golpea,
si soplaras en mi corazón, cerca del mar, llorando,
sonaría con un ruido oscuro, con sonido de ruedas de tren con
    sueño,
como aguas vacilantes,
como el otoño en hojas,
como sangre,
con un ruido de llamas húmedas quemando el cielo,
sonando como sueños o ramas o lluvias,
o bocinas de puerto triste,
si tú soplaras en mi corazón, cerca del mar,
como un fantasma blanco,
al borde de la espuma,
en mitad del viento
como un fantasma desencadenado, a la orilla del mar, llorando.

Como ausencia extendida, como campana súbita,
el mar reparte el sonido del corazón,
lloviendo, atardeciendo, en una costa sola:
la noche cae sin duda,
y su lúgubre azul de estandarte en naufragio
se puebla de planetas de plata enronquecida.

Y suena el corazón como un caracol agrio,
llama, oh mar, oh lamento, oh derretido espanto
esparcido en desgracias y olas desvencijadas:
de lo sonoro el mar acusa
sus sombras recostadas, sus amapolas verdes.

Si existieras de pronto, en una costa lúgubre,
rodeada por el día muerto,
frente a una nueva noche,

BARCAROLLE

If you should merely touch my heart,
If you should merely put your mouth upon my heart,
Your dainty mouth, your teeth,
If you should put your tongue like a red arrow
There where my dusty heart is beating,
If you should blow upon my heart, while near the sea and weeping,
Then it would sound with a vague noise, like the sound of wheels
    of a sleepy train,
Like vacillating waters,
Like autumn with its leaves,
Like blood,
With a noise of wet flames that burn the sky,
With sounds like dreams or branches or the rain,
Or horns within a mournful harbor;
If you should blow upon my heart, while near the sea,
Like a pale, white phantom,
At the border of the foam,
Amidst the wind,
Like a phantom that has been unchained, upon the sea-shore,
    weeping.

Like an extended absence, and like a sudden bell,
The sea distributes all the sounds the heart is making;
Now raining, growing dark, upon a lonely coast,
Night undoubtedly is falling,
And its melancholy blue of a banner in a shipwreck
Is peopled with some planets of hoarse silver.

The heart is sounding like a bitter shell;
Call out, O sea, O lament, O melted dread
Dispersed in dire misfortunes and in broken waves:
The sea accuses of sonorousness
Its leaning shadows, its green poppies.

If you should suddenly exist upon a gloomy coast,
Surrounded by the day already dead,
And facing a new night,

llena de olas,
y soplaras en mi corazón de miedo frío,
soplaras en la sangre sola de mi corazón,
soplaras en su movimiento de paloma con llamas,
sonarían sus negras sílabas de sangre,
crecerían sus incesantes aguas rojas,
y sonaría, sonaría a sombras,
sonaría como la muerte,
llamaría como un tubo lleno de viento o llanto,
o una botella echando espanto a borbotones.

Así es, y los relámpagos cubrirían tus trenzas
y la lluvia entraría por tus ojos abiertos
a preparar el llanto que sordamente encierras,
y las alas negras del mar girarían en torno
de ti, con grandes garras, y graznidos, y vuelos.

¿Quieres ser el fantasma que sople, solitario,
cerca del mar su estéril, triste instrumento?
Si solamente llamaras,
su prolongado son, su maléfico pito,
su orden de olas heridas,
alguien vendría acaso,
alguien vendría,
desde las cimas de las islas, desde el fondo rojo del mar,
alguien vendría, alguien vendría.

Alguien vendría, sopla con furia,
que suene como sirena de barco roto,
como lamento,
como un relincho en medio de la espuma y la sangre,
como un agua feroz mordiéndose y sonando.

En la estación marina
su caracol de sombra circula como un grito,
los pájaros del mar lo desestiman y huyen,
sus listas de sonido, sus lúgubres barrotes
se levantan a orillas del océano solo.

Replete with waves,
And you should blow upon my heart made cold with fear,
Should blow upon the lonely blood within my heart,
Should blow upon its movement of a pigeon fraught with flames,
Then its black syllables of blood would sound,
And its incessant reddish waters would increase,
And it would sound, would sound like shadows,
It would sound like death,
It would call as a pipe would that is full of wind or weeping,
Or as a flask that pours out dread in torrents.

So it is, and lightning would envelop all your tresses,
And rain would enter through your open eyes
To prepare the weeping that you secretly restrain,
And the black wings of the sea would flap about you,
With enormous claws and cawing sounds and flights.

Do you desire to be the phantom that solitary, blows
Beside the sea its sad and sterile instrument?
If only you would call
Its sound that is prolonged, its whistle so maleficent,
Its command of wounded waves,
Someone would come perhaps,
Someone would come,
Down from the summits of the islands, up from the red depths of
  the sea,
Someone would come, someone would come.

Someone would come; blow with fury;
Let it sound like the siren of a broken ship,
Like a lament,
Like a neighing in the midst of foam and blood,
Like a ferocious water biting itself and sounding.

In the nautical station
Its shell of shadows is revolving like a shout;
The birds upon the sea reject it, fleeing;
Its stripes of sound, its mournful bars
Are rising on the shores of the lonely ocean.